7/7

The Key

to Understanding

the Gospel of

John

7/7: The Key to Understanding the Gospel of John

ISBN 978-1-955295-01-7

 COURIER PUBLISHING

Greenville, South Carolina

PUBLISHED IN THE UNITED STATES OF AMERICA

DEDICATION

I dedicate this book to my wife, Joy,
my soul mate and partner in ministry for almost sixty years.

ENDORSEMENT

For nearly 25 years I had the honor and privilege of calling Dr. Ken Clayton — or "Bro. Ken," as he is more commonly known by those who love and admire him — "pastor and friend." Bro. Ken had the unique ability to preach God's Word in a simple manner that left you feeling like you had walked out of a Bible class. You learned fresh insights while at the same hearing the biblical truth that the gospel of Jesus Christ is available to all who believe in Him, ask for forgiveness, and repent of their sins. His ministry reflected his love for Jesus and the desire that everyone he met would eventually come to know Jesus as Savior.

Bro. Ken's insights on the Book of John are a must-read for all believers. His book, *7/7: The Key to Understanding the Gospel of John*, is a clear, concise compilation of the gospel that most Christians refer to as "must reading" for all Christians — but especially new believers. The book is divided into seven themes, thus making it an easy-to-read, yet thorough examination of the Gospel of John.

Lonnie Wilkey, Editor
Baptist and Reflector
Franklin, Tennessee

TABLE OF CONTENTS

PREFACE

In August 2019, I felt led of the Lord to preach a series of sermons on the Gospel of John. While in seminary in the 1960s, I was in a class on John taught by Dr. William Hull. It was a verse-by-verse in-depth study. This study was invaluable in developing these sermons. As I was praying and preparing for the sermons, I realized there are a series of "seven sevens" in John. I knew there were seven signs and seven "I Am Who I Am" sayings of Jesus. I realized there were seven other sevens.

ACKNOWLEDGMENTS

My thanks to the loving family that is called Pine Eden Baptist Church. They were very understanding and patient with me, as many of these sermons were web-cast during the current COVID-19 pandemic. Also, in 2019, Joy suffered five strokes and was in the hospital or rehab for seven months. Since that time, she has been doing rehab and recovering at home. During all this time, I was not able to serve full time at Pine Eden. We will always be grateful for the prayers, love, and support of the church.

7/7

The Key
to Understanding
the Gospel of
John

Ken Clayton

CHAPTER 1

THE 7 THEMES
JOHN 1:1-3, 14, 18, 34

THE 1ST THEME: JESUS IS THE SON OF GOD

The first century world was flooded with ideas, similar to our twenty-first century. Matthew, Mark and Luke, led by the Holy Spirit, presented overviews of Jesus' life. When John wrote his gospel, he selected events and words of Jesus for one main purpose: that people might find eternal life by believing Jesus is the Christ, the Son of God. So the first theme is that Jesus is one with God.

That is one reason John's gospel is so important today. We tend to apply our faith to Sunday and religious occasions, but leave it behind in the public world. John presents Jesus as our bridge between what is spiritual and our everyday human world. Jesus is the Word of God, but He took on flesh and dwelt among us (John 1:1, 14). Jesus can show us how our faith is relevant in our day-to-day lives.

WHO WAS JOHN?

John's father was Zebedee and his mother was probably Salome. He had a younger brother, James. They were commercial fishermen, living in Capernaum, near the Sea of Galilee. The name John means "*Yahweh is* gracious." John was one of Jesus' disciples and became part of the inner circle of Peter, James and John. At first, John must have been a hothead. In Mark 3:17, Jesus called the brothers "sons of thunder"! Once, they wanted to call down fire on a Samaritan village. On another occasion, they almost caused a riot among the disciples when they wanted to sit on either side of Jesus in the kingdom (Mark 10:35-45).

But Jesus changed John's life. He became known as "the disciple whom Jesus loved" (John 13:23). John has been called the "apostle of love" because the theme of love is frequent in his writings. Because of Jesus, the "son of thunder" became the "son of love." John went on to write the Gospel of John, three New Testament letters and Revelation.

'IN THE BEGINNING' (V. 1)

The first theme in John's gospel — and the most important — is that Jesus is one with God. God has revealed Himself in three ways: As God the Father, God the Son, and God the Holy Spirit. Genesis 1:1 says, "In the beginning God created the heavens and the earth." John declared that "in the beginning," the Word was present with God, and *was* God! That Word *is* Jesus (1:14). John is saying that Jesus was there before creation. Jesus is eternal. Jesus was not just a good man, a good teacher, or a miracle worker. Jesus is eternal with God — which means that God was, and is, always like Jesus.

'... WAS THE WORD' (V. 1)

The Jews believed "Word of God" in the Old Testament meant the mind of God. The Greeks believed the "word" was the creating power of God. So John wrote to Jews and the Greco-Roman world that Jesus Christ is the creating mind of God who came to earth. People no longer had to wonder about God — all they had to do was look at Jesus and see who God is!

'WORD WAS WITH GOD ...' (VV. 1-2)

There has always been the most intimate connection between the Word (Jesus) and God. No one can tell us what God is like, what God's will is for us, or what God's love, heart and mind are like, as Jesus can! Jesus has always been with God. So only Jesus can reveal what God is like. "I and my Father are one" (John 10:30).

'WORD WAS GOD' (V. 1)

Jesus said in John 14:11, "Believe Me that I am in the Father and the Father in Me." There is a oneness that is difficult for us to understand. Jesus is the same in character, mind, quality and being as God. Jesus is so perfectly the same as God that, in Jesus' life and teaching, we perfectly see what God is like! So right in the beginning of his gospel, John declared that in Jesus, and Jesus alone, there is perfectly revealed all that God always was, and is, and always will be.

'ALL THINGS WERE MADE ...' (V. 3)

The Word — Jesus — is the Creator of all things. "All things were made through Him, and without Him nothing was made that was made" (v. 3). Why would John so emphasize Jesus and creation?

In John's day, there were the false teachings of the Gnostics. This false teaching was even in some churches. In order to explain sin, evil, sorrow and suffering in the world, the Gnostics came up with a new story of creation. They taught that in the beginning there was God and matter — and that all matter was evil, and out of the evil matter a power came that was horrible to God. That evil power created the world. So the world was evil, and their bodies were evil. So the Gnostics believed they could do anything with their evil body, and it did not affect their standing with God.

John wanted his readers to know the truth about creation. This happened a long time ago. So why is it important today? It helps us understand why Satan continues to attack the biblical account of creation. People who believe in evolution or the Big Bang Theory deny God as Creator. Paul wrote in Colossians 1:16: "For by Him were all things created that are in heaven and that are in earth … . All things were created by Him and for Him." In 1 Corinthians 8:6, Paul said of Jesus, "by Whom are all things," and in Hebrews 1:2 "the Son by whom God made the world."

GOD CREATED OUT OF NOTHING

Genesis 1:2 includes the phrase that says "the earth was without form and void" — which means there was "nothing." There were also no flaws in God's creation. Genesis 1:4, 10, 12, 18, 21, 25, and 31 declare that "God saw that it was good." This is our Father's world!

Evil exists because of man's rebellion and disobedience to the Word of God. Disobedience began with Adam and Eve, and continues to this day. Jesus was one with God in creation, and Jesus was one with God in redemption. Because of Jesus' death on the cross and His resurrection, He has redeemed all who will believe. We have been recreated — born again (John 3:16) — and one day Jesus will recreate all things: "Now I saw a new heaven and a new earth, for the first heaven and the first earth had passed away. … 'Behold, I make all things new'" (Revelation 21:1 and 5).

THE WORD BECAME FLESH (JOHN 1:14)

This is one of the most important verses in the New Testament. This verse is why John wrote his gospel. The truth of this verse changed history. Without the truth of this verse, we would all still be lost in our sin. The powerful and creative Word of God became human! The "Word became flesh and dwelt among us" (John 1:14). The word "dwelt" means to "pitch a tent." Jesus came, "and we beheld His glory." The word "beheld" in verse 14 is used twenty times in the New Testament and always means "actual physical sight." So the Son of God became really human, and John really saw Him. The Greco-Roman world believed that the body was evil. Paul described the "flesh" as our human nature in all its sin. Some false teachers in the early church called themselves "Docetists," because they taught that Jesus just seemed to be a human. Many have had a difficult time believing Jesus came in the flesh. John attacked these heresies directly in 1 John 4:2-3. Jesus was fully God and fully man. Jesus showed us how God would have lived the life we live.

John then said, "We saw His glory, the glory as of the only begotten of the Father." The word "glory" is used for the presence of God. The glory of God was seen in the cloud and the fire that guided the Israelites in the Exodus (Exodus 16:10). The glory of God was on Mt. Sinai (Exodus 24:16), and His glory filled the tabernacle (Exodus 40:34). The term "glory" describes Jesus in John 2:11, 5:41, 7:18, 8:50, 54, 11:4 and 17:5.

In verses 14 and 18, Jesus is described as the "only begotten of the Father." The phrase "only begotten" can mean "unique" or "specially loved." Jesus is unique, and the phrase "in the bosom of the Father" shows the deepest sense of closeness. Jesus and the Father are one. Only Jesus can "declare" or reveal the true nature of God.

THE 2ND THEME: LIFE (JOHN 1:4)

How many of you have seen a television program or a movie about the Lone Ranger? The distinctive music in the Lone Ranger productions is the William Tell Overture, which is the overture to the opera "William Tell," composed by Rossini in 1829. A composer would begin by playing the themes of the music that would be reflected in the whole work. This is exactly what John did. "In Him was life and the life was the light of men" (John 1:4). The word "life" appears forty-four times in John's gospel. John's gospel begins and ends with "life."

Life was found in Jesus. John's purpose in writing was that people might "believe that Jesus is the Christ, the Son of God, and that believing you might have life through His name" (John 20:31). In John 5:40, Jesus said, "But you are not willing to come to Me that you may have life." Jesus said, "I have come that they may have life, and that they may have it more abundantly" (John 10:10). And in John 10:28, "I give them eternal life, and they shall never perish, neither shall anyone snatch them out of My hand." Remember, Jesus said, "I am the way, the truth, and the life" (John 14:6).

WHAT DOES JOHN MEAN BY LIFE?

Life is the opposite of destruction, death, judgment and hell:

"... that whosoever believes in Him would not perish, but have everlasting life" (John 3:16).

"... believes in Him who sent Me has everlasting life, and has not come into judgment, but has passed from death to life" (John 5:24).

And in Chapter 5, verse 29, John contrasts the resurrection to life and the resurrection to condemnation. Jesus gives us security. Until you accept Jesus and take him as Savior and enthrone Him as your King, you are not alive at all! You exist, but you don't know what life is. Jesus alone makes life worth living. In Jesus' death is a transition to eternal life. "And this is the will of Him who sent Me, that everyone who sees the Son and believes in Him may have everlasting life, and I will raise him up at the last day" (John 6:40).

WHAT KIND OF LIFE IS THIS?

What does "eternal life" mean? It is not simply this kind of life that lasts forever. The word John uses for "eternal" is the same word used repeatedly to describe God. Only God is eternal! So eternal life is the life which God lives. What Jesus offers us is God's own kind of life. Eternal life has the peace and power of the life of God Almighty.

HOW DO YOU ENTER ETERNAL LIFE?

We enter by believing in Jesus Christ. The world "believe" occurs seventy-nine times in the Gospel of John. "He that believeth on Me, has everlasting life" (John 6:47). But true belief involves accepting Jesus' commands and a willingness to do anything He challenges us to do.

THE 3RD THEME: LIGHT (JOHN 1:4-9)

"And the life was the light of men." The third great theme is "light," which is used in John's gospel twenty-four times.

The function of John the Baptist was to point people to the light that was in Christ (John 1:6-9). Twice, Jesus called Himself the "light of the world" (John 8:12, 9:5). In John 11:10, the light can be seen by men so that they can become "children of light" (John 12:36). Jesus said, "I have come as a light unto the world" (John 12:46).

WHAT DID JESUS MEAN BY USING THE IDEA OF LIGHT?

1) Light brings order out of chaos. In Genesis 1:3, God moved upon the dark, formless chaos and said, "Let there be light." With light, God swept away chaos. Jesus is "the light that shines in the darkness" (John 1:5). One of our fears is the fear of the dark. Left by ourselves, without Jesus, we are in the darkness of our sins and doubts and fears — our personal chaos.

2) The light of Jesus is a revealing light. "That light has come into the world, and man loved darkness rather than light ..." (John 3:19). Men love darkness because their deeds are evil, and they "do not come to the light, lest their deeds should be exposed" (John 3:20). Jesus' light reveals us for who we really are. Jesus exposes our disguises and our phoniness. Our response should be sorrow and repentance.

3) *The light of Jesus is a guiding light.* If you do not have the light of Jesus, you are walking in the darkness (John 12:35) and "you don't know where you are going" (John 12:36). "I have come as a light into the world, that whosoever believes in Me shall not abide in darkness" (John 12:46). Your time of doubt and uncertainty can be over. Come to Jesus. Your dark path can be flooded with light.

THE 4TH THEME: WITNESS (JOHN 1:7-8, 5:32-39)

What is a witness? By definition, a witness is "a person who saw an event take place," and "a person who has knowledge of an event or person, from personal experience or observation." Now in a court of law, there are "expert" witnesses — persons who are trained professionals that might give medical opinions or DNA evidence, for example.

"Witness" is the fourth theme found in John's gospel. The word "witness" is found twenty-one times in John's gospel. In John 1:7-8, John the Baptist is described as a witness to the light of Jesus three times.

JOHN THE BAPTIST

John was a prophetic voice. For 400 years, the voice of prophecy had been silent. John the Baptist, a prophetic voice, "came for a witness to bear witness of that light" (John 1:7). John could witness that he saw the Spirit descending upon Jesus (John 1:32). "And I have seen and testified that this is the Son of God" (John 1:34). In John 1:29, John the Baptist publicly witnessed to all who were present, saying, "Behold! The Lamb of God who takes away the sin of the world." In John 5:32-33, four times the word "witness" is used in connection with John's testimony about Jesus.

THE WITNESS OF JESUS' WORKS (JOHN 5:36)

"The works that I do in my Father's name, they bear witness of Me" (John 10:25). Jesus told Philip, "Believe Me that I am in the Father and the Father in Me, or else believe Me for the sake of works themselves" (John 14:1). Jesus condemned those who had seen His works and did not believe (John 5:24). The witness of Jesus' works was not just His miracles, but His whole life. Jesus' works were all the things He said and did. It was how He lived His life. His was a life of love, mercy, compassion, forgiveness and service. The only way Jesus could live that kind of life was if He was truly the Son of God.

THE WITNESS OF GOD THE FATHER (JOHN 5:37)

"The Father who sent Me bears witness of Me" (John 8:18). Jesus had no doubt who He was and who sent Him. At Jesus' baptism, John the Baptist "saw the Spirit descending from heaven" (John 1:32).

THE WITNESS OF THE SCRIPTURES (JOHN 5:39)

"For if you believed Moses, you would believe Me: for he wrote about Me" (John 5:46). Jesus fulfilled all of the 121 prophecies about the coming Messiah. All the Jewish hope for a Messiah was finalized in the coming of Jesus.

THE WITNESS OF JESUS HIMSELF (JOHN 8:14)

"I am One who bears witness of Myself, and the Father who sent Me bears witness of Me" (John 8:18). Jesus claimed to be life and light and truth and the way. Jesus claimed to be the Son of God and one with the Father. He claimed to be Savior and Lord: Jesus' life, character, and resurrection proved all those claims to be true. If anyone else had said these things about themselves, it would be blasphemy. Jesus is who He said He is!

The Witness of Ordinary People

There were also ordinary people who testified about Jesus. Some examples are Nathanael (John 1:49); the women at the well in Samaria (John 4:39); the man born blind who was healed by Jesus (John 9:25); and the people who saw Jesus raise Lazarus from the dead (John 12:17). In every generation, there are many who have been ready to bear witness to the saving power of the Lord Jesus Christ.

The Witness of the Disciples

Jesus commissioned His disciples with these words: "You also shall bear witness because you have been with Me from the beginning" (John 15:27). John was a personal witness, and he wrote, "This is the disciple who testifies of these things, and wrote these things; and we know that his testimony is true." Matthew, Peter, John and James were eyewitness writers. Most scholars believe that Mark recorded much of his gospel with information from Peter. Luke traveled with Paul and knew Peter, Matthew, Mark and John.

The Witness of the Holy Spirit

"But when the Helper comes, whom I shall send to you from the Father, He will testify of Me" (John 15:26). And in 1 John 5:6, John wrote, "It is the Spirit that bears witness, for the Spirit is truth." The Holy Spirit brings God's truth and helps us recognize that truth. The convicting power of the Holy Spirit on our hearts gives us the opportunity to open our hearts to Jesus and believe in Him as the Son of God.

The last witness I call to your attention is ... YOU!

Will you testify to the grace of God poured out on your heart by the shed blood of Jesus on Calvary's cross? Will you testify of Jesus' forgiveness, love, and compassion for you? Will you testify that because of Jesus you know where you are going after death? Will you testify of His power and presence in your life everyday?

Can I get a witness? Who will testify? Will you join your testimony with millions of believers who have gone before you, that Jesus is King of kings and Lord of lords?

The 5th Theme: Believe (John 1:12-14, 16-17)

The way we come into a relationship with Jesus Christ and have eternal life is by believing in Jesus Christ as Lord and Savior. The word "believe" occurs seventy-nine times in John's gospel. Jesus said, "He that believeth on the Son shall have everlasting life" (John 3:36).

What does 'believe' mean?

One must be convinced that Jesus is truly the Son of God. If Jesus is only a man, why should we obey Him? We must believe He is the Son of God. But "believe" is more than intellectual acknowledgment that Jesus is who He says He is. We must accept His commandments and do what He teaches us in His Word. So "believe" has three components:

1) We must be convinced in our minds that Jesus is the Son of God, our Savior.

2) We must trust in our hearts that everything Jesus has said is true.

3) We must obey Jesus in all that we do, because He is King of kings and Lord of lords.

CHILDREN OF GOD

In John 1:11, John stated that His own people rejected Jesus. "But as many as received Him, to them He gave the right to become children of God, to those who believe on His name" (John 1:12). When we believe in Jesus, we are adopted into the family of God. We can't enter the family by our own will or power. God — through His grace (John 1:14, 16) — opened the way to Himself through Jesus. God offers us the right to become His children. But some reject the offer. We can accept the offer by believing in Jesus. We can be born again (John 1:13) — not by bloodlines, not because we made a way (the will of man), but because God opened the door.

"And of His fullness we have all received, and grace for grace" (John 1:16). In Colossians 1:19, Paul said, "All the fullness of God dwelt in Jesus Christ." When we believe in Jesus, fullness comes to us. The Holy Spirit comes to dwell in our hearts, "grace for grace."

The question is, where are you? Are you among the rejectors of Jesus or the believers in Jesus?

THE 6TH THEME: TRUTH (JOHN 1:14, 17)

JESUS IS TRUTH

Jesus is full of "grace and truth" (John 1:14). In John 14:6, Jesus said, "I am [Who I Am] the way, the truth and the life." To discover truth, you must look to Jesus. Another dominant theme in John's gospel is truth. Jesus told the disciples that if they stayed with Him, they would "know the truth" (John 8:11). Jesus told Pilate, "I have come into the world, that I should bear witness to the truth. Everyone who is of the truth hears My voice" (John 18:37). The truth makes us "free" (John 8:32).

TRUTH AND THE HOLY SPIRIT

Jesus said He would send His Spirit to tell the truth and guide us to the truth. Jesus' Spirit is the Spirit of truth (John 14:17, 15:26, 16:13). "The law was given through Moses, but grace and truth came through Jesus Christ" (John 1:17). The word "truth" appears twenty-seven times in John's gospel.

THE 7TH THEME: FEAST

FEAST

The seventh theme in John's gospel is the word "feast." Although this word is not found in the first chapter of John, it is used to show the reason Jesus came to Jerusalem alone. John shows us more clearly than the other gospels that Jesus traveled to Jerusalem to worship and celebrate the feasts of Israel with other Jews. The center of Jesus' ministry seemed to be in the Galilee region. But Jesus came to Jerusalem at feast times. The word "feast" occurs twenty-one times in John's gospel.

THE FEASTS AND JERUSALEM

"After this there was a feast of the Jews and Jesus went up to Jerusalem" (John 5:1). John's outline of Jesus' activities in Jerusalem begins with the mention of a feast. In John 2:13, John mentions Passover — and Jesus cleansed the temple, taught the people, and met with Nicodemus. Another example is in Chapter 7, verse 2: "Now the Jews' Feast of Tabernacles was at hand." Jesus talked with His brothers, taught the people, was rejected by the religious authorities, and proclaimed, "I am [Who I Am] the light of the world" (John 8:12). The Feast of Tabernacles was also called the "Feast of Lights," because Jerusalem was filled with lights, and there was a joyous feast much like our Thanksgiving.

The feasts are the outline of Jesus' movements from the Galilee region to ministry in Jerusalem. The other six themes are important key ideas that help our understanding of who Jesus is, what He taught, and what He did.

CHAPTER 2

THE FIRST 7 DAYS
THE FIRST WEEK OF JESUS' EARTHLY MINISTRY

In John 1:19, John begins the narrative section of his gospel. In the beginning, John laid out the themes he would develop in the rest of his account of Jesus' life and ministry. Now John presents a day-by-day narrative of the first week of Jesus' public ministry.

DAY 1 (JOHN 1:19-28)

What if someone asked you to write down your life story? Now if you wrote in a day-by-day diary fashion, your life story would fill many volumes. John did not attempt to record everything Jesus said or did (John 21:25). Led by the Holy Spirit, John chose events and words of Jesus that clearly demonstrated that Jesus is the Son of God.

Interestingly, when John began to write about Jesus, he described the events of the first week of Jesus' ministry. John's description of this first day began when a delegation of priests and Levites were sent to John the Baptist to interrogate him. The phrase "the Jews" occurs seventy times in John and is the name used for those who opposed Jesus. So from the beginning, John's gospel portrayed the opposition and rejection of Jesus by the Jewish religious authorities.

THE JEWS HAD LONG LOOKED FOR THE MESSIAH

John the Baptist confessed that he was not the Messiah (John 1:20). John also denied that he was Elijah (John 1:11). The Jews believed that before the Messiah came that Elijah would return. They also asked if he was "the prophet." Moses had said that God would raise up a prophet like him and they were to listen to him (Deuteronomy 18:15). Again, John said no. Again, they asked, "Who are you?" (John 1:22). John answered with a quote from Isaiah 40:3 that explained that his task was to prepare the way for the Messiah.

IF JOHN WAS NOT ONE OF THESE IMPORTANT PEOPLE, WHY WAS HE BAPTIZING PEOPLE? (JOHN 1:25)

An Israelite was not baptized. Baptism was for people coming into Judaism. But John was baptizing Jews, which meant that John believed the Jewish people needed to repent and be cleansed. John changed the focus from himself to the Messiah. John was just using water, "but there stands One among you whom you do not know" (John 1:26). By this time Jesus had already been baptized by John, and John had seen the Spirit descend upon Jesus. John testified of this experience in John 1:32-34. John said he was not worthy to untie Jesus' sandal strap (John 1:27). Taking off sandals was the lowest slave task. John knew that Jesus was the Messiah, and it is possible that Jesus was nearby, because John said He "stands among you" (John 1:26).

DAY 2 (JOHN 1:29-34)

John 1:29 begins: "The next day ... ." So this is day two. John saw Jesus and proclaimed, "Behold! The Lamb of God who takes away the sin of the world" (John 1:29). John applied a common image to Jesus to explain who Jesus was. The "Lamb of God" would have reminded the people of the Passover Lamb. When the Israelites were in Egyptian bondage, the Lord told them to sacrifice a lamb and put its blood around the door of their dwelling. The blood was a sign for the death angel to pass over that home. This was the Lord's last plague on Egypt to force them to release Israel. One day, the blood of Jesus would make possible the forgiveness of sin, and God's judgment would pass over the obedient faithful.

THE IMAGE OF A LAMB

This image should have reminded the Jews of the sacrificial lamb that was offered every morning and every evening in the temple for the sins of the people (Exodus 29:36-42). Jesus is the sacrificial lamb slain on Calvary's cross. Twenty-nine times in the Book of Revelation, the precious title "Lamb of God" is used for Jesus. The title sums up Jesus' love and sacrifice.

John declared for all present that day that he had seen the Spirit descending as a dove when Jesus was baptized (John 1:32). John proclaimed that Jesus is the Son of God (John 1:34).

DAY 3 (JOHN 1:35-39)

John 1:35 begins: "Again, the next day ... ." On the third day of Jesus' public ministry, His first two disciples came to Jesus and desired to follow Him.

Two of John the Baptist's disciples heard him say, "Behold the Lamb of God." They were looking for the coming of the Messiah, and this designation John the Baptist used for Jesus led them to believe that Jesus was the promised Messiah. So they left John and followed Jesus (John 1:36-37). Jesus asked, "What do you seek?" They called Jesus "Teacher" and asked where He was staying. This indicated they wanted to stay with Jesus and learn from Him (John 1:38). Jesus responded, "Come and see," so they followed Jesus that day (John 1:39).

Day 4 (John 1:40-42)

One of the two who followed Jesus was named Andrew (John 1:40). He found his brother Simon and brought him to Jesus (John 1:41-42). Note that Andrew announced to Simon, "We have found the Messiah." Andrew seemed to be convinced and wanted his brother Simon to meet Jesus. What a momentous event! The man who would become the leader of the disciples was introduced to Jesus by his brother.

Besides bringing Simon to Jesus, the events in Scripture surrounding Andrew concern his introducing people to Jesus. Andrew brought a boy with loaves and fish to Jesus (John 6:8-9), and later be brought some Greeks to Jesus (John 12:22). We may not become a great leader like Peter, but we can all be like Andrew and introduce people to Jesus.

When Jesus met Simon, Jesus changed his name to *Cephas,* which, in Hebrew, means "rock." The Greek name for "rock" is *Petros,* or Peter.

Day 5 (John 1:43-51)

More disciples

John stated that on "the following day," Jesus called Philip to "follow Me" (John 1:43). Then Philip found Nathanael and invited him to meet Jesus (John 1:45). Philip believed Jesus to be the Messiah. Nathanael was skeptical and said that nothing good could come out of Nazareth (John 1:46). When Jesus met Nathanael, He told Nathanael two things:

1) *He was a "true Israelite," the type of person God desired (John 1:47).*

2) *Jesus said He saw him "under the fig tree" (John 1:48).*

Nathanael's great confession

The most important of John's themes — and one of the primary reasons for writing his gospel — was to declare that Jesus is the Son of God. So here, early in John's narrative, Nathanael declared, "You are the

Son of God, you are the King of Israel" (John 1:49).

It is vital that we put voice to our beliefs. It is more than mere words when it comes from our hearts. (Romans 10:9-10)

DAY 6 (JOHN 1:43)

Day 6 was probably a travel day. In verse 43, John wrote, "Jesus wanted to go to Galilee … ." Apparently that is what happened.

DAY 7 (JOHN 2:1-12)

Verse 1 begins, "On the third day … ." Two days prior, Jesus had met Nathanael — and now on the third day, Jesus, the disciples, and Jesus' mother were all invited to a wedding in Cana of Galilee (John 2:1-2).

JEWISH WEDDINGS

Jewish laws stated that weddings should take place on a Wednesday. Although the celebration could last for a week, the ceremony itself took place late in the evening after a feast. The couple would be taken through the streets with a torch-lamp parade to their house. They would have open house for a week and would be like a king and queen. Drunkenness was a disgrace, but hospitality required wine. To the Jews, wine represented life and abundance.

NO MORE WINE

When the wine ran out, the mother of Jesus told Him (John 2:3). Whatever we face in life, whether it seems to be a small problem or a large challenge, we need first to tell Jesus. Jesus responded, "My hour has not come …" (John 2:4). The phrase "Jesus' 'hour'" is mentioned several times in John's gospel. "Jesus' 'hour'" would come on the cross. Jesus' life was all about doing His Father's will and in His Father's timing. So by faith, Jesus' mother told the servants to do whatever Jesus said (John 2:5).

THE FIRST SIGN

On the seventh day, Jesus performed what John called a "sign" (John 2:11). There were six large water pots available that were used for purification, or ceremonial washing (John 2:6). The hands and feet of the servants would have been washed. They each would hold between twenty to thirty gallons of water. Jesus told the servants to "fill them" and "draw some out" and "take it to the master of the feast" (John 2:7-8). The master of the feast would be like a wedding coordinator today. He was amazed — "saved the best for last" (John 2:9-10) — for the water had become wine. After the wedding, Jesus, His mother, brother and disciples went to Capernaum (John 2:12).

CHAPTER 3

THE 7 SIGNS

The purpose for John in writing his gospel is that he wanted his readers to know: "Jesus is the Christ, the Son of God, and that believing [they would] have life in His Name" (John 20:31).

John recorded seven signs that pointed to the truth that Jesus is the Son of God. The number seven is important. In the Bible, the number seven signified perfection or completion. Each of these seven signs are rooted in the Old Testament understanding of the coming Messiah. John's point is that Jesus is perfect and complete and that Jesus fulfills the Old Testament prophesies about the Messiah.

THE 1ST SIGN (JOHN 2:1-12)

We have already noted this first sign that occurred on the seventh day of Jesus' first week of public ministry. When Jesus turned the water into wine, He "manifested His glory" (John 2:11). That is, Jesus demonstrated the personal presence of the Lord. This sign revealed that Jesus is the source of real life, abundant life, eternal life. Jesus is Lord over matter.

This first sign of Jesus points to some wonderful truths:

1) *Jesus always wants the best for us and He knows what is best.*

2) *The six water pots would have contained between 120 to 180*

gallons of water. What an abundance of wine! Nothing can exhaust the grace of the Lord. "Now to Him who is able to do exceedingly abundantly above all that we ask or think, according to the power that works in us" (Ephesians 3:20).

3) It is not a crime to be happy. A wedding was the most happy time in Jewish life. There is a time to be serious, but our faith should not make us grim, unhappy, and somber people.

4) Jesus saved a young couple from a small village the hurt and humiliation of running out of wine. Jesus' love and care extends to the least of us and to the smallest detail.

5) This was more than a miracle, it was a sign that Jesus is the Son of God (John 2:11).

John chose certain events and teachings of Jesus to help his readers know who Jesus is. What you and I choose to do or say will help or hinder other people from coming to know and understand who Jesus is. What activities will you choose not to do that would dishonor Christ? What activities will you choose to do that would honor Christ and further His kingdom? Are you busy serving yourself or your King?

THE 2ND SIGN (JOHN 4:46-54)

HEALING A NOBLEMAN'S SON

The word translated "nobleman" (John 4:46) in Greek was used for a royal official, probably a person of high standing in King Herod's court. Jesus was in Cana. Capernaum was twenty miles away. This high official had to humble himself to travel to Cana and beg a carpenter-traveling preacher-healer to help his son (John 4:47). His son was at the point of death. His dignity, class, wealth, nor position stopped him from going to talk to Jesus. He didn't care what people thought, he went to Jesus and "implored" (begged) Jesus to heal his son.

When we need help, we must turn to Jesus. We must humble ourselves, swallow our pride, not caring what people think or say, and go to Jesus.

NOBLEMAN WAS NOT DISCOURAGED

Jesus seemed to be blunt when He responded, "Unless you believe and see signs and wonders, you will by no means believe" (John 4:48). Jesus was drawing out of this man what he really believed. More important than a physical healing was whether or not this man really believed in Jesus. If the nobleman had become irritated or proud, he might have turned away, revealing he had no faith in Jesus. No pretender will be accepted by Jesus.

NOBLEMAN'S FAITH

He begged Jesus to "come down before my child dies" (John 4:49). Jesus responded, "Go your way, your son lives ... . The nobleman believed the word that Jesus spoke ..." (John 4:50). Real faith believes what Jesus has said. At times we may wish His words were different or were vague. The only way to know the peace of believing is to believe that Jesus' words are true. Jesus is Lord over distance.

RESULT

As he was traveling, his servants met him and told him, "Your son lives" (John 4:51). The question "when?" was answered by the servants: The fever left at the seventh hour (John 4:52). The nobleman knew that was when Jesus had said, "Your son lives." So he believed and so did his whole household (John 4:53).

In light of this powerful miracle at a distance of twenty miles, they believed. It must have been mind-boggling that a carpenter from Nazareth was the Messiah. It must not have been easy for an official of King Herod's court to believe in Jesus, but he did. He experienced what

Jesus could do. John declared that this was the "second sign Jesus did" (John 4:54).

THE 3RD SIGN (JOHN 5:1-17)

JEWISH FEASTS

In verse 1, John wrote, "A feast of the Jews, and Jesus went up to Jerusalem." There were three Jewish feasts that every adult man who lived within twenty miles of Jerusalem was required to attend — Passover, Pentecost, and Tabernacles. This feast could have been Tabernacles, since Passover is mentioned in Chapter 6. John pointed out that Jesus traveled to Jerusalem for the feasts to worship His Father, along with other Israelites.

POOL OF BETHESDA

Jesus seemed to be alone when He came to this famous pool. Bethesda means "house of mercy." The word for "pool" comes from the word for "to dive." So it must have been a deep pool. Apparently there was an underground stream that occasionally bubbled up. People believed an angel disturbed the water, and the first person in the water would be healed (John 5:2-4).

A MAN LAME FOR THIRTY-EIGHT YEARS

Jesus chose to talk with probably the worst case there. Jesus asked, "Do you want to be made well?" (John 5:6). That was a good question. Perhaps his hope had died. Some people prefer to have no responsibilities. They prefer to drift through life. What if Jesus asked you, "Do you want to be changed?" How would you answer? The man explained to Jesus that he had no one to help him into the pool in time when the water was disturbed (John 5:7). His answer was simply, "Yes, I do, but I can't do it."

JESUS, LORD OVER TIME

"Rise, take up your bed and walk" (John 5:8). Would the man take Jesus at His word? Would he believe? The word translated "bed" is pallet. The man obeyed! He walked! Many things in life may defeat you, but life is not hopeless. We have Jesus! One day we will be in His presence. Jesus is Lord over time.

RESULT

The man, lame for thirty-eight years, walked. Notice that Jesus is compassionate for the man's condition, but also concerned for where he will spend eternity. Jesus said, "You have been made well. Sin no more ..." (John 5:14).

The second result is pointed out by John repeatedly. "For this reason the Jews persecuted Jesus, and sought to kill Him, because He had done these things on the Sabbath" (John 5:16).

Other passages about the Jewish religious leaders' rejection of Jesus are: Jesus cleansed the temple (John 2:13-22); the Jews questioned John the Baptist (John 3:22-36); many disciples turn away (John 6:60-71); whole chapter of rejection (John 7:1-52); Abraham's seed and Satan (John 8:37-59); effort to stone Jesus (John 10:31-39); and the plot to kill Jesus (John 11:45-57).

These passages all occur before the events of Jesus' last week of public ministry. John makes it clear that the religious leaders were opposed to Jesus and plotted all the time to seek to destroy Jesus.

We all face difficult situations. It may not be illness. But whatever is troubling you, turn it over to Jesus. Seek His forgiveness. Seek His presence, seek His love. If you really want to, you can do that right now. Come to Jesus.

The 4th Sign: Feeding The Five Thousand (John 6:1-14)

"After these things ..." (John 6:1). Jesus had been in Jerusalem and had healed a man lame for thirty-eight years. There followed conflict with the Jewish authorities who "sought to kill him" (John 5:16). After the hostilities and the teaching of Jesus recorded in Chapter 5, Jesus returned to Galilee.

A great multitude sought out Jesus because of "His signs which He performed on those who were diseased" (John 6:2). There were times when Jesus withdrew from the crowds in order to rest, pray, and teach His disciples (John 6:3). Jesus crossed over to the other side of the "Sea of Tiberias." John used this name, instead of the "Sea of Galilee," for his Greek readers.

The crowd had seen the direction of Jesus' boat, and so they walked around the north end of the sea and crossed the Jordan. This was a nine-mile trip. This is the most traveled route for Jews going to Jerusalem from the north. They would travel south and cross the Jordan River near Jericho and go up to Jerusalem. They traveled this route to avoid going through the hated Samaritan area, which was directly south of Capernaum.

Many in the crowd may have been traveling to Jerusalem to celebrate Passover and stopped in order to see Jesus (John 6:4).

What to do?

Jesus saw the multitude and had compassion for them, so He asked Philip, "Where shall we buy bread?" (John 6:5). It was natural to ask Philip since he was from a small village near the northern ford of the Jordan River (John 1:44). This was a test, because Jesus knew what He was going to do (John 6:6). Would Philip respond with faith? Philip calculated that 200 *denarii,* or six months wages for a working man, could not buy enough bread (John 6:7). We often calculate instead of living by faith. We only think about our resources or what we are able to do. We often leave Jesus out of the equation. Nothing is impossible with the Lord! Trust Jesus!

ANDREW

Andrew always played second fiddle to his brother Peter. "Andrew, Simon Peter's brother ..." (John 6:8). It's amazing what can be accomplished in the Lord's work when we don't worry about who gets the credit! Andrew again was bringing someone to Jesus, a boy with five barley loaves and two small fish (John 6:9). That would have been great, but Andrew kept talking. He just had to add: "... but what are they among so many?" (John 6:9). So many of us have the same problem — we don't know when to stop talking. Introducing this boy to Jesus was great, but Andrew showed a lack of faith by thinking "this is impossible."

Now barley bread was the cheapest bread, the bread of the very poor. The boy had five small, pancake-size pieces of bread. There were many types of small fish in the Sea of Galilee that were caught and pickled. Jesus was given a boy's lunch.

JESUS' INSTRUCTIONS

First, Jesus had the people sit down, and there were five thousand men (John 6:10). Jesus took the loaves and gave thanks. In the Jewish family the father said the blessing for the food. The prescribed blessing was, "Blessed art Thou, O Lord, our God, who causes bread to come forth from the earth." Then Jesus gave the bread to the disciples so they could distribute it to the people. The same was done with the fish, "as much as they wanted" (John 6:11). In verse 12, John stated that "they were filled." The word for "filled" is where we get our word "glutton." They ate more than they needed. Jesus then told them to "gather up the fragments."

They gathered up twelve baskets. None was wasted (John 6:13).

Results

A small lunch fed five thousand, until they were full, with twelve baskets left over. This demonstrated abundance. Jesus' grace and love are abundant. Jesus would go onto say, "I am [Who I Am] the bread of life" (John 6:35). This was John's listing of the first of Jesus' seven "I Am Who I Am" sayings. The idea that the feeding of five thousand was a sign is mentioned in John 6:26 and 30.

When the people had seen the sign that Jesus did, they said: "This is truly the Prophet who is to come into the world" (John 6:14). Jesus knew the people wanted to make Him king, just because He fed them. So Jesus left (John 6:15). They had seen the sign, but only saw it as a hope of fulfilling their physical needs and missed the powerful spiritual truth that Jesus was the Son of God. They missed that Jesus is the bread of life.

THE 5TH SIGN: WALKING ON WATER (JOHN 6:15-21)

Jesus left the crowd

Jesus also left the disciples and went off by himself further up the mountain above (John 6:15). The disciples went down to the sea and got into a boat, and it was dark (John 6:16-17). Matthew wrote that Jesus told the disciples to get in the boat and go to the other side while He dismissed the crowd and went up the mountain to pray (Matthew 14:22-33).

The Storm

While crossing over to Capernaum, it became dark (John 6:17). "A great wind" began blowing and the sea had high waves (John 6:18).

Mark, in writing of that storm, said that disciples were in the "middle of the sea." Jesus saw them straining at rowing against the wind (Mark 6:45-52).

WALKING ON THE WATER

Then the disciples saw Jesus walking on the sea, coming to their boat, and they were "afraid" (John 6:19). Mark added that they thought it was a ghost. Jesus called out to them: "It is I, do not be afraid" (John 6:20). In Matthew's gospel, Peter asked to go to Jesus. Jesus invited Peter to come. Peter looked at the wind, became afraid, and began to sink. Peter cried out, "Lord, save me!" When we are in trouble, we need to cry out to Jesus.

Peter didn't appeal to the other disciples, nor did he try to swim. He called out to Jesus (Matthew 14:28-31). When Jesus entered the boat, the storm ceased and the boat was at the shore (John 6:21).

THE MEANING OF THIS SIGN

John wanted his readers to know that Jesus is Lord over nature. Jesus can walk on water, Jesus can calm the storm, and Jesus can still the wind and the waves. Since Jesus can control nature, Jesus is in control of all things. Jesus can calm the storms, the stress and anxieties in your life. Jesus can overcome the waves of despair, hurt, loneliness, and trouble that seem to wash over you.

In every storm, trust Jesus. When you need comfort in sorrow, strength in difficulty, peace in turmoil, no one can help like Jesus.

But we must ask ourselves: Do we want Christ's gifts without Christ's cross? Do you want to use Jesus instead of allowing Jesus to use you?

Where do you stand today in your relationship with Jesus? He will save you. Commit your heart and life to Jesus now.

THE 6TH SIGN: HEALING THE MAN BORN BLIND (JOHN 9:1-12, 25, 34-41)

The sixth sign in John's gospel that clearly pointed to the truth that Jesus is the Son of God was Jesus giving sight to a man born blind. This is the only healing miracle in the gospel of someone afflicted from birth.

THE MAN BORN BLIND

Jesus and the disciples had just left the temple area in Jerusalem (John 8:59). As they walked, they passed a blind man (John 9:1). Blindness was common in those days. There were many flies that carried diseases that infected eyes. It seemed that the disciples knew this man (John 9:2).

1) The disciples asked, "Who sinned?" Some Jews believed that you could sin in your mother's womb. Greek pagans believed in the preexistence of the soul. Some Jews adopted this pagan view and believed that some people were good or bad when born. This is totally a non-biblical view! Some Jews believed that a person could be punished for the sin of their parents. The Old Testament does teach that the sin of parents can affect their children (Exodus 20:15, 34:7; Numbers 14:18; Psalm 109:14).

2) Jesus' response: "Neither, but that the words of God be revealed in him" (John 9:3). The miracles of Jesus were signs of the glory and power of the Lord. When we are faced with affliction, sorrow, pain, or loss, we can demonstrate to the world how a faithful person can live trusting in Jesus.

3) The teachable moment: This event gave Jesus an opportunity to explain that we need to seize the day — to use wisely the time the Lord has given us (John 9:4).

4) A powerful truth: The blind man gave Jesus an opportunity to declare a powerful truth. Jesus declared, "I am [Who I Am] the light of the world" (John 9:5).

THE HEALING

Jesus spat on the ground and made a clay paste and put it on the man's eyes (John 9:6). Jesus told the man to go wash in a specific place — the Pool of Siloam. The man obeyed Jesus exactly, and he was healed (John 9:7). His neighbors, in disbelief, questioned him. He told his neighbors what Jesus had done (John 9:8-12).

THE JEWISH INQUISITION

The neighbor took the man to the Pharisees (John 9:13). It was the Sabbath when Jesus healed the man — also, making the clay paste would have been work and so would healing on the Sabbath (John 9:14). The Pharisees asked him how he had received his sight and he told them (John 9:15). The Pharisees were divided in their judgment. Some judged Jesus as not being from God because He did not keep the Sabbath. Others felt that if Jesus were a sinner, He could not "do such signs" (John 9:16). The Pharisees questioned the man again, and they questioned his parents. The parents gave a minimal answer: He is our son, and he was born blind. They said, "He is of age, ask him" for they were "afraid" (John 9:17-23). The angered Pharisees again confronted the man and commanded the man to tell the truth in the presence of God: "This man is a sinner" (John 9:24). So they questioned him again in verse 26. The man became bolder and asked if they wanted to be Jesus' disciples (John 9:27). The man began to teach the Pharisees. (1) You don't know where He is from, and He healed my eyes. (2) God only hears those that worship Him. (3) It is unheard of that a man born blind would be healed. (4) He must be from God (John 9:28-33). So the angry Pharisees excommunicated the man (John 9:34).

TRUE BLINDNESS

Jesus found the man. Jesus came "to seek and save the lost" (Luke

19:10). Jesus questioned the man, "Do you believe in the Son of God?" (John 9:35). The man asked, "Who is he?" and basically Jesus answered, "I Am" (John 9:36-37). The man declared, "Lord, I believe!" (John 9:38). Jesus declared that He had come for the specific judgment of revealing that those who are blind may be able to see, and those who think they can see, their blindness will be revealed. The Pharisees realized Jesus was referring to them. Jesus confirmed their realization and added, "You say, 'We see.' Therefore your sin remains" (John 9:39-41).

The growing testimony

1) The man's first testimony was just the facts: "a man" healed him (John 9:11).

2) His second testimony was again just the facts (John 9:15).

3) His third testimony was that "He is a prophet" (John 9:17).

4) His fourth testimony was that "once I was blind, but now I see" (John 9:25). He began to defend Jesus.

5) His fifth testimony was that He was a "Man from God" (John 9:33).

6) His sixth testimony was "Lord, I believe!" (John 9:38).

Three lessons

1) The more we know Jesus, the greater He will be to us.

2) There will always be Pharisees. There are those people who are legalistic kill-joys whose religion is doom and gloom, who will doubt and question your faith. It is because they do not know the giver of sight to the blind or the giver of salvation to those who believe and the giver of heaven to the faithful.

3) Just as Jesus searched and found the man born blind, He is searching for you. Do you want to be found? Do you want to be healed?

THE 7TH SIGN: LAZARUS RAISED FROM THE DEAD
(JOHN 11:1-27, 38-44)

The number seven was a symbol of perfection or completion. The seventh sign in John's gospel was raising Lazarus from the dead. This sign pointed to the truth that Jesus is the Son of God, as Martha declared, "Yes, Lord, I believe that You are the Christ, the Son of God, who is to come into the world" (John 11:27). The seventh sign demonstrated that Jesus has power over death!

CRY FOR HELP

This whole event started with a cry for help. Jesus had a close relationship with the family of Mary, Martha, and Lazarus. Their home was a welcome refuge from the hostility of the Jewish religious authorities. "Now Jesus loved Martha and her sister and Lazarus" (John 11:5).

The name Lazarus means "God is my help." So when Lazarus became ill, the sisters sent for Jesus (John 11:3). Jesus told the disciples that this had happened "for the glory of God, that the Son of God may be glorified" (John 11:4). In John's gospel, the ultimate glory of Jesus would be revealed in the cross and resurrection of Jesus. The presence and power of the Lord would be revealed. The raising of Lazarus from the dead was the last sign before the cross.

THE DELAY

It may seem strange that Jesus delayed two whole days after receiving the news about Lazarus (John 11:6). Jesus always took action in His own timing. So often we want Jesus to do things on our time schedule, but we must leave everything to His timing. Then Jesus told the disciples, "Let us go to Judea again" (John 11:7). The disciples were concerned because they knew that the Jews wanted to kill Him (John 11:8).

Teachable moment

Jesus seized this moment to teach His disciples. There are only "twelve hours in a day," Jesus said. That time cannot be extended and should not be wasted. While you have the light, you won't stumble (John 11:9). But if you try to walk in the night, you will stumble (John 11:10).

John uses "dark" and "night" to describe life without Jesus Christ (John 13:30). Jesus is the light of the world and while Jesus was present, they needed to come to the light and walk in the light.

Then, after some discussion, Jesus told the disciples plainly, "Lazarus is dead" (John 11:14). Jesus knew this sign would grow their faith (John 11:15). Then Thomas showed great courage when he said, "Let us also go, that we may die with Him" (John 11:16). "Thomas" was his Jewish name. Thomas' Greek name was "Didimus," or "twin." Often remembered as "Doubting Thomas," it should also be remembered as "Courageous Thomas." Real courage is being aware of the danger, but doing the right thing in spite of the danger.

Jesus arrived in Bethany

When Jesus arrived, Lazarus had been in the tomb for four days (John 11:17). Since Jerusalem was only about two miles from Bethany (John 11:18), there were many Jews there comforting the sisters (John 11:19). When Martha heard that Jesus was coming, she rebuked Him for not arriving sooner (John 11:20-21). But Martha also declared one of the greatest statements of faith in the New Testament: "But even now I know that whatsoever You ask of God, God will give You" (John 11:22).

Jesus assured Martha of the resurrection of Lazarus (John 11:23). Martha did believe in the resurrection "at the last day" (John 11:24). Then Jesus announced the essential truth of the gospel, "I Am the resurrection and the life. He who believes in Me, though he may die, he shall live." The vital question for Martha and for us is, "Do you believe this?"

(John 11:25-26).

Death is not the end. We call this the "land of the living." It is really the "land of the dying." When we know Jesus as Lord and Savior, we pass from the land of the dying to the land of the living.

When Mary met Jesus, she responded in much the same way as did Martha (John 11:28-32) with a hurt rebuke.

THE REACTION AND ACTION OF JESUS

Mary was weeping and the Jews were weeping, and Jesus "groaned in the spirit and was troubled" (John 11:33). The "groaning" was evident of deep emotion in Jesus. The Greeks believed their gods had a total inability to feel any emotion. Their gods were isolated and passionless. Jesus revealed that God cares and that God has compassion and is moved by our troubles and sorrows (John 11:35-36). Notice there was always criticism from the Jews (John 11:37).

When Jesus approached the tomb, it was a common burial method, a cave with a stone across the opening. Again, Jesus "was groaning in Himself" (John 11:38). Jesus commanded that the stone be removed from the tomb opening, but Martha protested, because the body would be in decay and there would be the stench of death (John 11:34). If you believe, you will see the powerful presence (glory) of the Lord (John 11:40). When the stone was rolled away, Jesus prayed. Jesus thanked the Father for hearing Him, as He always did. Jesus prayed all of this out loud because He wanted the people to believe that God had sent Him (John 11:41-42).

Then Jesus commanded the dead man, "Lazarus, come forth!" (John 11:43). Lazarus came out still wrapped with grave clothes and Jesus commanded those standing by to "loose him and let him go" (John 11:44).

The reaction of the people

Some believed in Jesus (John 11:45). Some reported this to the Pharisees. They were perplexed as what to do. Jesus had done many "signs" (John 11:47). So "they plotted to put Him to death" (John 11:53) and they sought Jesus to seize Him (John 11:52).

Some important lessons

1) We cannot control God. Our Lord acts in His timing, responding to us according to His plans. Jesus is on time, all the time.

2) Jesus is filled with love, compassion, and deep feelings for our hurts, sorrows, and troubles.

3) Jesus is the resurrection and the life for all who believe that Jesus is the Son of God. Jesus has the power over death (1 Corinthians 15:55, 57).

4) The raising of Lazarus from the dead was a powerful sign. On the day of Jesus' triumphal entry into Jerusalem, one of the reasons for the large crowd was the testimony of those who had seen Jesus raise Lazarus from the dead (John 12:17-18). John saw this sign as the greatest sign that pointed to the truth that Jesus is the Son of God. The people came "because they heard that He had done this sign" (John 12:18).

CHAPTER 4

THE 7 'I AM WHO I AM' SAYINGS

JOHN 8:25-30, 53-59

Another key to understanding John's presentation of his gospel of the Lord Jesus Christ are the seven "I Am Who I Am" sayings of Jesus. These sayings are vital to our understanding of who Jesus is and why He came. But before we come to the sayings, we must know their background. In order to understand, I want to go back to the encounter of Moses with the Lord in the burning bush.

MOSES AT THE BURNING BUSH (EXODUS 3)

Moses was tending the sheep of Jethro, his father-in-law, in the area near Mt. Sinai. Moses saw a bush burning, but not being consumed. Moses drew closer and encountered the presence of the Lord. The Lord called his name: "Moses, Moses" (Exodus 3:4).

The great climax of the encounter was when Moses asked God's name. God answered, "I Am Who I Am" (Exodus 3:14). The Hebrew consonants "YHWH" stood for *Yahweh*. By Jesus' day, the Jews were afraid to pronounce the name of the Lord, so when they saw the name in the Scripture they said *Adonai* (LORD) instead.

JESUS' CONFLICT WITH THE JEWS

From the early days the Jewish religious leaders were opposed to Jesus. In John 8, Jesus was teaching in the temple. He told His opponents that they would die in their sins because they did not believe "I Am Who I Am" (John 8:24). The word for "sin" means "to shoot an arrow at a target and miss." The person who refuses to believe in Jesus has missed the target in life. The essence of sin is that it separates a person from God. The cure for sin is to believe that Jesus is the Son of God and to follow Him in obedience.

THE JEWS ASKED, 'WHO ARE YOU?'

Jesus responded that he had told them from the very beginning who He was (John 8:25). The Jews problem was not mentally misunderstanding what Jesus had been saying about Himself; it was a heart blindness. They were so determined to keep their religion their way, to maintain the system they owned and operated, that they closed their eyes to the truth. Human nature has not changed. There are people today who have a heart blindness to who Jesus is.

Jesus' response is recorded in verse 28. They would realize the truth when Jesus was lifted up on the cross to pay the penalty for sin. The cross of Jesus still speaks powerfully to people today about the love and forgiveness of Jesus. The cross would make clear that Jesus is the "I Am Who I Am." Jesus was claiming to be the Lord God Almighty! Jesus told them that the Father had sent Him. And the things that Jesus said and did were because the Lord was with Him and He "always did those things that please Him" (John 8:28-29).

THE JEWS ASKED, 'WHO DO YOU MAKE YOURSELF OUT TO BE?' (JOHN 8:53)

This exchange began in verse 48 when the Jews accused Jesus of having a demon. Jesus denied that and said He was honoring His Father (John 8:49). Jesus made a startling claim: "If anyone keeps My Word, he shall never taste death" (John 8:51).

They were positive then that Jesus had a demon because everyone dies, even Abraham and the prophets had died (John 8:52). So who are you? (John 8:53). Jesus then clearly began to tell them who He is:

1) *You call Him God, I call Him Father (John 8:54).*

2) *I know Him, you don't (John 8:55).*

3) *Your father is Abraham, My Father is God (John 8:56).*

4) *Before Abraham was, "I Am Who I Am" (John 8:58).*

When Jesus claimed to be God, the Jews took up stones to kill Him, and Jesus hid Himself and left (John 8:59). Jesus claimed to be timeless; He was before Abraham. There never was a time when He was not. The human person Jesus was born into this world at Bethlehem. But as it is written in Hebrews, Jesus is "the same yesterday, today, and forever" (Hebrews 13:8). There is only One who is timeless; only One who created time; and only One who can say "I Am Who I Am." That is God! Jesus' claim is that He is God who came to earth. He is "Emmanuel — God with us."

In Jesus, we see the timeless God, who was the God of Abraham, Isaac, and Jacob. Our God was before time, who will be after time, who always is. In Jesus, the eternal God showed Himself to the world. Jesus is the great "I Am Who I Am"!

SAYING 1: 'I AM WHO I AM — THE BREAD OF LIFE' (JOHN 6:30-58)

When the Lord revealed His name to Moses from the burning bush, His name indicated the vital truth that the Lord is always present. There never has been a time when the Lord was not present. If you could visualize a yardstick as all of time from start to finish, the Lord could be standing back observing all history. But the Lord is not aloof or far off and disinterested in us as most world religions picture their gods. I believe the most important theme in the Bible is when the Lord declared many times, "I am with you." The Lord is connected at all points along the "yardstick" of history. For example, He walked with Adam and Eve in the garden of Eden; He told Abraham, Isaac, Jacob, Joseph, Moses, Joshua, David and many others in the Old Testament, "I am with you." Then He came in the person of Jesus who is "Emmanuel — God with us." Jesus told the disciples, "I am with you always ..." (Matthew 28:20). The rest of the New Testament is a testimony of the work of the Holy Spirit in the church. At the end of history — the end of the "yardstick" — Jesus will come again.

THE SIGN — FEEDING FIVE THOUSAND

Jesus fed five thousand men with a boy's lunch. Jesus had compassion on the multitude and fed them until they were all full (John 6:12). Then the disciples took up twelve baskets full of leftover food (John 6:13).

THE REACTION

1) Because of the miraculous feeding, many people began to seek Jesus (John 6:22-24). Jesus told the people that they sought Him not because they understood the sign, but that they were fed (John 6:26).

2) The people responded, "What shall we do, that we may work the works of God?" (John 6:28). Jesus answered, "This is the work of God, that you believe in Him whom He sent" (John 6:29).

3) Then the people said, "What sign will you do that we may believe you?" (John 6:30). Moses gave manna in the desert over a period of time (John 6:31). Jesus answered My Father gave the manna, not Moses. God is the giver of the true bread from heaven. The true "bread of God is

He who comes down from heaven and gives life to the world" (John 6:32-33).

4) The people took Jesus literally and wanted to be fed always (John 6:34). Jesus' response was: "I am [Who I Am] the bread of life ..." (John 6:35). Jesus took the personal name of God revealed to Moses in the burning bush and applied it to Himself. He claimed that those who came to Him would never hunger and those who believed would never thirst (John 6:35). This powerful promise was made to those who believe. Jesus added that those who come to Him will not be turned away (John 6:37). Their problem was that they did not believe (John 6:36). Jesus said that He had come to do His Father's will. The Father's will was that all who believe in Jesus will have everlasting life (John 6:38-40).

I AM WHO I AM — THE BREAD OF LIFE

In light of all the discussion about manna, Jesus again reminded the people of His outstanding claim. That He is the Lord, the bread of life. The people began to murmur among themselves because they knew Jesus was the son of Joseph and they knew His mother also (John 6:42). They refused to believe, because they thought they knew Jesus' human ancestry. Jesus knew what they were murmuring (John 6:43) and explained that the heart of the matter is believing in Him (John 6:43-47).

Then for the third time, Jesus told them that "I am [Who I Am] the bread of life" (John 6:48). The people who ate the manna in the wilderness were all dead. Jesus is the living bread which came down from heaven. The one who eats this bread will never die, but live forever. The bread Jesus would give was His flesh for the world (John 6:49-51).

THE JEWS QUARRELED AMONG THEMSELVES

The Jews' lack of faith led them to take Jesus literally again. Jesus explained that a person needed to eat His flesh and drink His blood. Doing that would mean that Jesus would abide in them and they would have eternal life (John 6:53-56). Just as Jesus lived because of the Father, those who feed on Jesus will live (John 6:57).

Jesus wants us to know that those who consume Him will have eternal life. The Lord commanded Jeremiah to eat the scroll. To consume the Word of the Lord. We must consume Jesus, take Him into our lives, so that Jesus lives in us and we in Him.

Jesus is the Word of God. As we consume Jesus, we take Him into our lives and He becomes real to us. We live with Jesus in our hearts.

THE LORD'S SUPPER IS A PICTURE OF THIS TRUTH

The Lord's Supper is a symbolic representation of what Jesus said. Jesus took bread and said, "This is my body given for you. Take and eat." Bread represents Jesus' body that died on the cross to pay the penalty for sin. He abides in us by faith. Jesus also took a cup and said, "This is my blood shed for the remission of your sins, all of you drink of it." The cup represents Jesus' blood shed on the cross for our sin. Jesus abides in us when we believe in His shed blood for us on the cross.

Have you tasted the love and grace of Jesus? Have you consumed His body and blood by faith into your heart and soul? Are you abiding in Jesus?

Jesus is the bread of life, and when Jesus enters your life, you will never taste the second death, eternal torment in hell.

SAYING 2: 'I AM WHO I AM — THE LIGHT OF THE WORLD' (JOHN 8:12-20, 25, 28-30)

The second "I Am Who I Am" saying of Jesus recorded in John's Gospel is "I am [Who I Am] the light of the world."

Light

The word "light" is found over 200 times in the Bible. The word often is associated with the Lord. In Genesis 1:2, "the earth was without form and void ... darkness was on the face of the deep." In Genesis 1:3, "God said, "Let there be light and there was light." It was not until verse 14 that it was stated, God said, "Let there be light in the firmament of heaven ... ." It was not until verses 15 and 16 that the sun and the moon were named. What was the light in verse 3? I believe it was the presence of the Lord! The last part of verse 2 said, "The Spirit of God was hovering over the face of the water." The Lord was present. Light — the glory of the Lord — was an indication of the presence of the Lord. Some examples:

1) *Fire in the burning bush.*
2) *Fire led the Israelites in the wilderness.*
3) *"The Lord is my light" (Psalm 27:1).*
4) *"The Lord gives light" (Proverbs 29:13).*
5) *"The Lord is a lamp unto my feet and a light unto my path" (Psalm 119:105).* "In Him was life and the life was the light of men" (John 1:4). "God is light ... walk in the light as He is in the light" (1 John 1:5, 7). "The city had no need of the sun or of the moon to shine in it, for the glory of God illuminated it. The lamb is its light" (Revelation 21:23).

Feast of Tabernacles

The three great pilgrim feasts of Israel were times to gather in Jerusalem in the temple to worship the Lord. The Feast of Tabernacles was celebrated in early October. It was a harvest festival. It was also called the "Feasts of Booths" because of the temporary shelters set up in the fields during the harvest. The workers could stay out in the fields to protect the harvest and work from sunup to sundown.

Even city dwellers build booths because the festival also symbolized the wilderness journey of Israel before they entered the promised land.

The Feast of Tabernacles was also called "The Festival of Lights." This was a joyous celebration, much like our Thanksgiving. All Jerusalem would be lit at night. The Jews had the "illumination" in the court of the women in the temple area. There was a large bronze bowl, twenty-four feet across that was filled with oil with a wick made of old rags. It would be lit that night and the men would sing praises to the Lord all night. "Tabernacles" is mentioned in John 7:2, 10, 37.

1) Feast: The seventh theme in John's gospel is "feast." John shows more clearly than the other gospels that Jesus came to Jerusalem at the various feast times. The word "feasts" is found twenty-one times in John's gospel. Jesus was in Jerusalem to celebrate the Feast of Tabernacles. In the midst of all the light Jesus declared, "I am [Who I Am] the light of the world!" (John 8:12). Jesus declared that He was *Yahweh* — the light of the world.

2) Court of the women: This was the larger outer courtyard of the temple area. It was also the area of the temple treasury (John 8:30). There was thirteen trumpet shaped containers with the small end up. People would be there putting in their offerings. Many faithful Jews would have heard what Jesus said.

3) Word: Being the light of the world means that Jesus' heart and salvation are available to anyone, anywhere, anytime. People can respond in faith to the offer of God's grace and be saved. Jesus was not just the light for the Jews or just some elect or select group, but for the world.

4) Follow Me: This term was used in four ways —

- Used of a soldier following his captain.
- Used of a slave following his master.
- Used of a citizen following the laws of the state.
- Used of a disciple following the precepts of a teacher. So a follower of Christ goes where he is commanded like a soldier.

And like a slave obeys every order given by his master, he obeys the laws and teachings of the Lord Jesus Christ.

REACTION

The religious leaders always reacted with rejection (John 8:13). They asked, "Where is Your Father?" (John 8:19). When Jesus told them He would go away (John 8:21), they asked, "Will He kill Himself?" (John 8:22). Again in verse 25, they asked, "Who are You?" Then in verse 28, Jesus gave them a clear and definitive answer: "When you lift up the Son of Man." When Jesus was lifted up on the cross, it would be possible for people to know that "I Am Who I Am." At the cross, a Roman soldier said, "Surely this is the Son of God" (Mark 15:39). At that point, they should realize that Jesus is the Christ, the Son of God. Jesus, to emphasize His statement, said that His Father had sent Him, but has not left Him alone (John 8:29). This is the same promise Jesus made to us. Jesus said, "I will never leave you nor forsake you" (Hebrews 13:5).

THE ILLUSTRATION

John gave us a great illustration that Jesus is the light of the world. One of the seven signs is found in Chapter 9, where Jesus healed the man born blind. Jesus declared, "I am [Who I Am] the light of the world" (John 9:5). Jesus not only healed the man physically, but also spiritually. Jesus later asked the man, "Do you believe in the son of God?" (John 9:35). When the man realized Jesus was talking about Himself, he cried out, "Lord, I believe!" (John 9:38).

Some of the Pharisees were offended when Jesus said that there were some who thought they could see, but were blind (John 9:39-41).

Where do you stand in your spiritual life? Are you like the man who was blind in his sin, but saw Jesus, believed and was saved? Or, are you like the Pharisees who believed they could see, but did not see who Jesus was, did not believe and remained in their sin? Without Jesus, you are blind. He is the light. Come to the light and see and know Jesus. Like the words of an old song, "I saw the light, no more darkness, no more night."

SAYING 3: 'I AM WHO I AM — THE DOOR' (JOHN 10:1-10, 15, 17-18)

We must remember that what is translated "I Am" is literally "I Am Who I Am," which is the English for the personal name God gave Moses in the burning bush. In Hebrew, the name is *Yahweh*. Seven times, Jesus used the name *Yahweh*, revealing who He is and giving a descriptive picture of what that meant. The third saying of Jesus is "I am [Who I Am] the door."

In the tenth chapter of John's gospel are interwoven two pictures: the picture of the door of the sheepfold, and the picture of a shepherd. In order to understand these pictures, it is necessary to know something of the geography of the land of Israel.

GEOGRAPHY

The majority of Judea is a plateau. It stretches about thirty-five miles north to south and from fourteen to seventeen miles east to west. The area is very rocky. The land is more suitable for raising sheep than it is for any large-scale farming. Since there is little grass and water, the sheep have to be moved often. The land drops off on both sides of the plateau and is dangerous country. A shepherd looking for a lost sheep discovered the caves of Qumran where the Dead Sea Scrolls were found. Qumran is a rocky desert-like area on the hills near the Dead Sea.

OTHER DANGERS

The sheep had to be protected from wild animals. In the Old Testament, David recalled defending the sheep against a lion and a bear. Another danger was thieves and robbers — "but climbs in some other way, the same is a thief and a robber" (John 10:1); "All who ever came before Me are thieves and robbers" (John 10:8); "The thief does not come except to steal, and to kill, and to destroy" (John 10:10). Using the sheep as an illustration, there were other dangers.

In Jesus' times, the dangers included false Messiahs. Revolutionists came declaring they were the Messiah, and they called for the overthrow of the Roman dominance over Israel. Among these groups were the zealots. Josephus, a Jewish historian, wrote that there were a multitude of disorders and revolts. There were also false teachers. There were Pharisees, Sadducees and other religious leaders who misrepresented God. Some were greedy, enjoying the wealth their religious system produced. They also enjoyed the power they had over the people. We live in a world that is filled with false teachers. Only in Jesus will we find the truth.

In the context of this situation, Jesus said, "I am [Who I Am] the door."

THE DOOR

"Enter the sheepfold by the door ..." (John 10:1). The shepherd was the only caretaker and protector of the sheep. The shepherd had two types of enclosures to help him.

1) Near the villages, there were community sheepfolds. When a shepherd was keeping his flock close to his village, he could bring his sheep into this sheepfold at night. This sheepfold had a real door with a doorkeeper. This would allow the shepherd to lead his flock in and out (John 10:1-3).

- Verse 1: "Door."
- Verse 2: "Shepherd enters the door."
- Verse 3: "Doorkeeper opens the door."

2) There were sheepfolds out in the hillsides away from the villages. They were walled, but had no door at the opening. So at night, the shepherd laid down across the opening. The sheep could not leave. A thief or wild animals would have to go over the shepherd. Literally, the shepherd was the door. No one could enter except through the shepherd.

WHAT WAS JESUS' MEANING?

1) Jesus declared His purpose in coming into the world was to lay down His life. Jesus came to die for us that we might be saved (John 10:15). He and His Father had worked out this plan.

2) In obedience, Jesus would lay down His life that He may "take it again" (John 10:17).

3) Jesus would do this willingly. He was not forced, it was His choice. Jesus had the power to "lay it down ... take it up again" (John 10:18).

4) Through Jesus alone, we have access to God. Paul wrote in Ephesians 2:18: "For through Him, we both have access by one spirit to the Father." In Hebrews 10:20, Jesus "is the new and living way." Through Jesus, we enter into the presence of the Father. Jesus is "the way, the truth and the life, no man cometh unto the Father except through Me" (John 14:6). You will never discover another way. Jesus is the door to the Father, the door to eternal life. "If anyone enters by Me, he will be saved," Jesus declared (John 10:9).

5) "... and will go in and out and find pasture" (John 10:9). The phrase "go in and come out" was a well-known expression in Hebrew. It was the Jewish way of describing a life that was safe and secure. We might say, "Come and go as you please." In Numbers 27:17, the leader of the nation is to be "one who can bring them out and lead them in." In

Deuteronomy 28:6, a person who is obedient to God is "blessed when he comes in and blessed when he goes out." In Psalm 121:8, God will keep him in his "going out and ... coming in." Only in Jesus do we have a sense of safety and security. In God's hands, there is no fear.

6) Abundant life is found in Jesus. In contrast to thieves who come to steal, kill, and destroy, Jesus came to give abundant life (John 10:10). To believe in Jesus and follow Jesus means you have an abundance of life, real life, eternal life. The word "abundant" means "surplus" or "filled and overflowing." When you walk with Jesus, Jesus fills your life. You will be living the kind of life the Lord wants you to live, and you will be ready to enter into the presence of the Lord.

Do you have the abundant life? Have you entered safely through the Door into eternal life?

SAYING 4: 'I AM WHO I AM — THE GOOD SHEPHERD' (JOHN 10:11-16, 27-31)

Probably the best-loved description of Jesus is that He is the Good Shepherd. This picture of the Lord as Shepherd is found in a number of places in the Old Testament. The word "Shepherd" is found sixty-five times in the Old Testament.

OLD TESTAMENT

This idea is referenced in Psalm 77:20, Psalm 79:13, Psalm 80:1, Psalm 95:7 and Psalm 100:3. "We are His people and the sheep of His pasture" (Psalm 100:3). Isaiah, describing the coming Messiah, wrote, "He shall feed His flock like a shepherd. He shall gather the lambs with His arm, and carry them in His bosom, and shall gently lead those that are young" (Isaiah 40:11). Jeremiah and Ezekiel both condemned the false shepherd leaderships in Israel (Jeremiah 23:1-11, Ezekiel 34).

Ezekiel 34 is the shepherd chapter. The Lord condemned the shepherd (national) leaders in Israel. Two important verses are 11 and 23. "For thus says the Lord God, 'Indeed I Myself will search for My sheep and seek them out'" (v. 11); "I will establish one shepherd over them, and He shall feed them — My servant David. He shall feed them and be their shepherd" (v. 23). This is a picture of the coming Messiah: one like David.

The Good Shepherd

In light of all the Old Testament references Jesus declared, "I am [Who I Am] the good shepherd" (John 10:11). When Jesus took upon Himself the picture of the good shepherd, what was He communicating to the people?

1) Jesus said He was "good." There were two words in Greek for "good." One simply means good moral quality. The second not only means good in moral quality but also a loving and lovely quality. The second Greek word is the one applied to Jesus. The word carries the idea of excellence in kindness, graciousness, and loveliness in Jesus.

2) Shepherd: Remember, the work of a shepherd is to guide the sheep to grass and water; to defend the sheep from wild animals and thieves; care for their wounds; and seek them when they are lost. The shepherd was always on duty. Jesus will never leave believers nor forsake them. Jesus guides, defends, cares, and seeks the lost.

3) Gives His life for the sheep: Jesus came to die on the cross and pay the penalty for our sin. Just as a shepherd in Israel would lay down across the opening to sheepfold, Jesus laid down His life for our salvation (John 10:11, 15, 17, 18).

4) Contrast: Jesus protects sheep, but the hireling does not (John 10:12-13). Someone who is just working for pay who really doesn't care for the sheep, flees when danger comes.

5) "I know My sheep" (John 10:14). The word "know" in the Bible means knowledge by experience, personally. Jesus has a personal relationship with His sheep, and the sheep know Jesus personally and intimately.

6) *"Gather other sheep" (John 10:16).* Jesus' flock was not just Israel, but the world (John 3:16). The "other sheep" is where you and I come in! Jesus will gather people from all over the world to "be one flock and one shepherd."

7) *Jesus is the leader (John 10:16).* Jesus said, "They will hear My voice." People will "hear My voice … know Me … they follow Me" (John 10:27). Sheep are led, not driven. Jesus leads His sheep. Those who follow Jesus receive eternal life (John 10:28). Eternal life is God's kind of life.

8) *Security (John 10:28):* Jesus said no one can "snatch them out of My hand." And in verse 29, "And no one is able to snatch them out of My Father's hand." That is real security. I picture Jesus putting His hand around me and the Father's powerful hand going around us. No one or nothing can snatch me away. Nothing can "separate us from the love of God which is in Christ Jesus our Lord" (Romans 8:39).

REACTION OF THE JEWS

Failure to believe: "Tell us if you are the Messiah or not" (John 10:24). Jesus replied, "I told you and you do not believe." They should have believed because of the powerful works that Jesus did (John 10:25).

The Jews wanted to stone Jesus (John 10:31). They accused Jesus of blasphemy, claiming Himself to be God, and they knew He was a man (John 10:33). In response, Jesus stated plainly, "I am the Son of God" (John 10:36). Then the Jews sought to seize Jesus (John 10:39).

Do you know the Good Shepherd? Not just the facts, but do you know Jesus intimately, personally? Are you following Jesus as Lord and Savior?

I had a professor in seminary who said that one day he saw a large flock of sheep with two shepherds near Jerusalem. When the shepherds came to a fork in the road, the shepherds parted and walked down two different roads. They began calling out names and the sheep began to divide into two flocks, each sheep following his shepherd. They heard their shepherd's voice and followed him.

Jesus is calling. Will you listen?

Saying 5: 'I Am Who I Am — The Resurrection and The Life' (John 11:17-27)

As Jesus approached Bethany (John 11:18), He was coming to visit His dearest friends. But Jesus had come on a sad occasion. Jesus had received word that Lazarus was seriously ill. Jesus delayed His arrival and when he arrived, Lazarus had been dead four days (John 11:17). Martha came out to meet Jesus. She rebuked Him, "If you had been here, my brother would not have died" (John 11:21). But then in faith she added: "I know that God will give You whatever You ask" (John 11:22). Then Jesus declared, "Your brother will rise again" (John 11:23).

Resurrection

In the Old Testament, there is practically no belief in life after death. There is a growing understanding of that truth as God opened their understanding in the Old Testament times. At first, the Jews believed that when a person died they went to *sheol*. *Sheol* was a vague, shadowing existence. "In death there is no remembrance of Thee; in the grave who shall give Thee thanks" (Psalm 6:5). "Shall Thy loving-kindness be declared in the grave, or Thy faithfulness in destruction? Shall Thy wonders be known in the dark? And Thy righteousness in the land of forgetfulness?" (Psalm 88:10-12). "The grave cannot praise

Thee, death cannot celebrate Thee; they that go down into the pit cannot hope for Thy truth" (Isaiah 38:18).

But even in the Old Testament times, there were glimpses of a growing understanding of God's plan. An example is Psalm 16:9-11: "My flesh also shall rest in hope; for Thou wilt not leave my soul in Sheol neither wilt Thou suffer Thine holy one to see corruption. Thou will show me the path of life; in the presence is fullness of joy; at Thy right hand there are pleasures forever more." The Jews began to talk about being "gathered to their father's" or to be in "Abraham's bosom" (Luke 16:22), then in Job 14:13-15 we see the real seed of the Jewish belief in life after death: "Oh, that You would hide me in the grave, that You would conceal me until Your wrath is past, that You would appoint me a set time and remember me! If a man dies, shall he live again? All the days of my hard service I will answer You." And in Job 19:25-27: "For I know my Redeemer lives, and He shall stand at last on the earth; and after my skin is destroyed, that I know, that in my flesh I shall see God, whom I shall see for myself, and my eyes shall behold, and not another."

By Jesus' time, the Pharisees and the majority of the Jews believed in the resurrection. But the Sadducees did not believe in life after death. With that background, Jesus declared:

'I Am Who I Am — the Resurrection …'

What did that statement of Jesus affirm?

1) There is a resurrection! All Sadducees and other doubters need to understand that this world is not all there is. There is life after death, Jesus said so!

2) Jesus is the resurrection (John 11:25). Jesus, being God Almighty, has the power of the resurrection. Jesus conquered sin, death, and hell and He is alive! Jesus is the only one who has the power over sin, death, and resurrection. He alone is able to give you entrance into life after death. Jesus demonstrated this truth when He raised Lazarus from the dead. The ultimate proof of the resurrection is that on the third day, after Jesus died on the cross and was entombed, He arose from the grave! Hallelujah! Jesus is the resurrection.

3) The key that opens the door of resurrection for us is to believe in Jesus. "He who believes in Me, though he may die, he shall live. And whoever lives and believes in Me shall never die" (John 11:25-26). Jesus then offered His listeners an invitation for them to express their faith by asking, "Do you believe this?" It is a matter of faith on our part. Jesus has done everything to provide salvation for us. The challenge is, do you believe this? Do you believe Jesus?

'... AND THE LIFE'"

What did Jesus mean when He declared, "I am [Who I Am] the life"?

1) Jesus conquered sin. When Adam and Eve sinned in the Garden of Eden, death entered. Today when a person refuses to believe and follow Jesus, they are dead in their trespasses and sins. "And you He made alive, who were dead in trespasses and sin" (Ephesians 2:1).

2) Jesus conquered death. When Jesus arose from the dead, He made it possible for us to conquer death as well (John 11:26).

3) Jesus gives life now. When we follow Jesus, He helps us live the life He has commanded us to live. Jesus promised, "I have come that they may have life, and that they may have it more abundantly" (John 10:10).

4) Jesus gives us a new relationship with God the Father. When you believe in Jesus, you believe what Jesus said about His Father. You believe that God is love, our Redeemer, and the giver of life. Because of that, the fear of death is gone.

5) Jesus gives life eternal. Physical death is not the end. "He that believes in Me, though he may die, he shall live" (John 11:25).

6) *The life that Jesus gives us is His kind of life.* It is eternal and filled with joy. John, in Revelation, recorded God saying: "There shall be no more death, nor sorrow, nor crying. There shall be no more pain, for the former things have passed away" (Revelation 21:4).

When we believe in Jesus, we are freed from the fear of death. We are freed from the fears that plague those who live a godless life. We are free in Jesus. We can look forward to our heavenly home. Are you possessed by fear or are you free in Jesus? Start today, start now, trust Jesus!

SAYING 6: 'I AM WHO I AM — THE WAY, THE TRUTH AND THE LIFE' (JOHN 14:4-6)

Jesus had repeatedly told the disciples that He would leave them and He told them where He was going. For example in John 7:33, "Yet a little while I am with you and then I go unto Him who sent Me." Jesus was going to the Father, but the disciples did not seem to understand. They did not understand the way Jesus was going, because it was the way of the cross.

Jesus told them not to be troubled because He was leaving them (John 14:1). Jesus' plan included preparing a place for them (John 1:3). Jesus challenged them to believe in Him (John 1:3). And in verse 4, Jesus declared, "You know the way." Thomas spoke up and said, "We don't know where you are going and we don't know the way" (John 14:5).

Thomas was too honest just to stand there and pretend he understood. He said what all the other disciples were probably thinking. The great outcome was that because of Thomas' statement, Jesus gave a wonderful answer. An answer that revealed more insight to us about who Jesus is and the power He possesses.

Jesus took three of the basic concepts of the Jewish religion and made the claim that He was the fulfillment of all three. Jesus declared: "I am [Who I Am] the way, the truth, and the life."

THE WAY

1) In the Old Testament, there are many passages that discuss the "way" a person must walk. Originally the word meant a literal path or road. It evolved to mean a person's conduct or lifestyle. The Old Testament also pointed out the ways of God. The word "way" is found 529 times in the Old Testament. The plural "ways" occur more than 200 times. In Deuteronomy 5:32-33: "You shall not turn aside to the right hand or to the left. You shall walk in all the ways which the LORD your God has commanded you … ." "Your ears shall hear a word behind you, saying, 'This is the way, walk in it" (Isaiah 30:21). And in Psalm 27:11: "Teach me Thy way, O Lord." With all of this Old Testament background, Jesus declared, "I am [Who I Am] the way."

2) In the New Testament, the Jesus movement was first called the "way" (Acts 9:2, 19:23, 22:4, 24:14, 22). Later, it was at Antioch that the followers of Jesus were called "Christians" (Acts 11:26). Jesus had taught that there were basically two ways to travel through life. One was the broad, easy way that led to death. The other was the narrow way, Jesus' way, that led to life (Matthew 7:13).

Years ago, when my wife, Joy, and I arrived in Valencia, Spain, to be missionaries, the plan was to learn Spanish in Spain. We began the process of settling in. That included finding an apartment, a language school, obtaining water, electric, gas and telephone service. One day I was walking around downtown looking for the telephone office. Using a phrase book, I was able to ask in Spanish, "Where is the telephone office, please?" The man I asked began to respond rapidly in Spanish, but realized I did not understand. So he motioned for me to follow him. We walked for blocks, making several turns, crossing the main central square. He walked up to an office entrance and opened the door and ushered me into the telephone office! He did not try to explain the way. He *was* the way. This is what Jesus does for us. He *is* the way. Jesus does not simply give us advice or point us in the right direction. He takes us by the hand and leads us. Jesus is the way!

When we witness to others to lead them to Christ, we can't just tell them the way. We have to be the way to Jesus.

THE TRUTH

Jesus said: "I am [Who I Am] the truth." The psalmist wrote: "Teach me Thy way; I will walk in Thy truth" (Psalm 86:11). "Thy loving-kindness is before my eyes and I have walked in Thy truth" (Psalm 26:3). Some people distort the truth, reasoning that whatever will benefit them is truth. However, Almighty God has given us His truth in His Word — the Bible. Jesus not only taught the truth, He personified the truth. Jesus is truth! The character of a person teaching math or geography might not affect their subject matter. But a person's character, his moral compass, does affect his outlook or the world, current events, relationships, and behavior. Real truth is not just conveyed in words; it finds expression in how you live.

Jesus is the only person who is the truth He taught. You and I might say, "I teach the truth." Only Jesus can say, "I am the truth."

THE LIFE

Jesus said, "I am [Who I Am] the life." We have discussed the concept of "life" several times in this series of sermons. "Life" is one of the key themes of John's gospel. The Scriptures have many references to "life." For example: "The reproofs of instruction are the way of life" (Proverbs 6:23). "He is in the way of life that keepeth instruction" (Proverbs 10:17). There are many passages that help us understand the work of

Christ. For example: "Thou will show me the path of life" (Psalm 16:11).

What all people are seeking is life. Real life. The search is for what will make life worth living. People have tried many different ways to find life. But life with Jesus is life worth living. It is real, true life.

What is the result of the statement of Jesus, "I am [Who I Am] the way, the truth, and the life"? The result is: "No one comes to the Father except through Me" (John 14:6). Jesus is the only way to God. In Jesus alone, we learn the truth about who God is and what He does. Jesus alone can reveal the Father. Jesus alone can bring you into the presence of God. Jesus alone opens the door to heaven. Jesus alone opens the door to eternal life.

Are you following the Way? The Way is Jesus. In following Jesus, you will know the truth — and you will have life.

Saying 7: 'I Am Who I Am — The Vine' (John 15:1-16)

In this passage, Jesus used pictures and ideas in a parabolic way. These pictures and ideas were interwoven in the religious heritage of Israel. Many times in the Old Testament Israel is portrayed as the vine or the vineyard of God. The word "vine," "vines," "vinedresser" and "vineyard" occur 159 times in the Old Testament. For example, a passage in Isaiah 5:1-7 is a passage of judgment on Israel, God's vineyard. Verse 7 says: "For the vineyard of the Lord of hosts is the house of Israel." "I had planted thee a noble vine" (Jeremiah 2:21). "Israel is an empty vine" (Hosea 10:1). The image of the vine was used so much it became the symbol of Israel. The temple had a golden vine on the front of the Holy Place. During the period of the Maccabees, the vine symbol was on their coins.

THE TRUE VINE

In light of all the vine imagery in the life and Scriptures of Israel, Jesus declared, I am [Who I Am] the true vine (John 15:1, 5). The word translated "true" meant "real, true and genuine." Why would Jesus make the claim that He was the genuine vine? In the Old Testament the picture of Israel as a vine is always used in a negative way. As a nation, Israel had received everything necessary to thrive, but they had failed as a vine of the Lord. The prophets pointed out how the nation had failed to stay connected to the Lord and productive in His service. By saying "true," Jesus was probably pointing out that Israel assumed that as the chosen people that they were automatically by birth a part of the Lord's vineyard. But it is Jesus who is the true vine. Just being a Jew would not save them. The only thing that would save them, or save you, is to believe in Jesus and have an intimate, personal relationship with the Lord Jesus Christ. Nothing will make you right with God except faith in Jesus.

THE VINEYARD

"And My Father is the vinedresser. Every branch in Me that does not bear fruit He takes away, and every branch that bears fruit He prunes, that it may bear more fruit." Jesus knew about vineyards. The vine was grown all over Israel. It took a lot of work to get the best fruit. The ground was cleared and the soil was prepared. Vines were planted about twelve feet apart. The young vines were cut back drastically so they might grow stronger. When the vine was mature, it had two types of branches — one non-fruit bearing and the other fruit bearing. The non-fruit bearing branches would be pruned to allow all the strength of the vine to go to the branches bearing fruit. The other branches would be burned (John 15:6).

The Judgment

Jesus used this image of the two branches to point out the two types of religious people. Some bear fruit and others do not. Who are these branches that don't bear fruit? Jesus was referring to the Jews who claimed to believe in God, yet they refused to believe in Jesus. I think this designation applies today to people who claim to be Christians, but don't live it. They have profession without practice, attendance without adoration, participation but no real praise. They have the form of religion, but not the faith in the Lord Jesus Christ. Are you listening to Jesus or just giving Him lip service?

The picture of judgment is seen in verse 2: "He takes away (destroys). In verse 6, "He is cast out ... is withered ... thrown into the fire and they are burned." Verse four states that a person cannot bear fruit apart from Jesus the real vine. The positive side of the judgment is seen in verse 2: "And every branch that bears fruit, He prunes, that it might bear more fruit."

Abiding in Jesus

Ten times in this passage, Jesus uses the word "abide." The word means "to take up residence or to dwell." The spiritual truth is that a Christian is in Christ, and Christ is in the Christian. This spiritual truth works in very practical ways:

1) Abiding in Jesus means we stay in constant contact with our Lord. This continual contact strengthens our lives and enables us to live the life we are called to live by our Savior. The secret of Jesus' life was His contact with His Father. So often Jesus withdrew to a quiet place where He could be alone with His Father. We must live every day aware of Jesus' presence with us. This means we will purposefully choose to spend time in worship, prayer, fellowship and meditation focused upon our Lord Jesus Christ.

2) Abiding in Jesus and in His words, we will be able to accomplish His purpose for our lives. This constant contact enables us to bear fruit (John 15:4), which means to be productive in the service of the Lord for the kingdom. We will be a faithful disciple. If we do not abide in Jesus, we will not accomplish anything of eternal value (John 15:5).

3) Abiding in Jesus is the key to an effective prayer life. Abiding in Jesus, being intimately connected to Jesus, means our hearts desire is to do His will. Your will is shaped by Jesus' will for you: "And it shall be done for you" (John 15:7). You will be praying that Jesus' will be done.

4) Abiding in Jesus glorifies our Heavenly Father and shows that we are Jesus' disciples (John 15:8). God is glorified when we bear fruit and others see our relationship to Jesus as His disciples.

5) Abiding in Jesus is the real love relationship (John 15:9). Jesus loves us in the same powerful and wonderful way the Father loves Him.

6) Abiding in Jesus depends upon our obedience (John 15:10). Jesus kept His Father's commandments and so abided in His love. The same will be given for us. As we abide in Jesus and keep His commandments, we will abide in His love. That is true in reverse: As we abide in His love, we will keep His commandments and continue to abide in Jesus.

7) Abiding in Jesus means we receive the joy of the Lord. Joy is greater than "happiness." Happiness depends upon happenings. Happiness is affected by many outside circumstances, many outside our control — like the current coronavirus pandemic. The joy of the Lord is our eternal possession (John 15:11).

8) Abiding in Jesus means that we love one another like Jesus has loved us. In keeping Jesus' commandments, we will fulfill all the others (John 15:12). Jesus wanted His disciples to understand the depth of His kind of love. Jesus demonstrated His love when He died on the cross to pay the penalty for our sin (John 15:13).

9) Abiding in Jesus, we are no longer servants, but friends. Jesus gave us an intimacy with God, so that we are not strangers, but intimate friends (John 15:14-15).

10) Abiding in Jesus means we are "chosen." Jesus has chosen or called us into this special relationship of a friend instead of a slave, so that we can bear fruit that will remain. It will stand the test of time. The only way to bring others into the Christian faith is to show them the fruit of your faith. Jesus has called us to send us out, "appointed you that you should go and bear fruit" (John 15:16).

Jesus has called us to become a part of the family of God. We are in an intimate relationship with Jesus as we abide in Him as a branch abides in the vine. We can take everything to the Lord in prayer. We are called into a special relationship of love that fills us with His eternal joy.

Have you entered into this special relationship? This relationship involves more than doing "churchy" things or following religious ceremonies. It means an obedience to the Lord's commandments, the greatest of which is to love one another.

Have you begun your journey with Jesus? You can start right now!

CHAPTER 5

THE 7 PEOPLE JESUS ENCOUNTERED

In the middle section of John's gospel (John 2:13-11:57), he records seven people who encountered Jesus. Again, the number "seven" means "perfect" or "complete." John had stated it was impossible to write down everything that Jesus did (John 21:25). So, led by the Spirit, John selected seven people to represent the many people with whom Jesus interacted.

As we come to the first person, we notice all seven of the themes that John emphasized in his gospel are involved in this encounter between Nicodemus and Jesus. For example, the seven are: Son of God (John 3:18); life (John 3:16); light (John 3:19); witness (John 3:11); believe (John 3:15); truth (John 3:21); and feast (John 2:23).

PERSON 1: NICODEMUS (JOHN 3:1-6)

THE TEMPLE

Jesus came to Jerusalem to observe Passover (John 2:13). Jesus came to the temple and found it filled with money changers and sellers of sacrificial animals (John 2:14). Jesus made a whip of cords and drove them out (John 2:15). Jesus exclaimed: "Do not make My Father's house a house of merchandise" (John 2:16). The Jews demanded a sign, a proof as to why Jesus had the authority to do this (John 2:18). Jesus declared:

"Destroy this temple, and in three days I will raise it up" (John 2:19). The Jews did not understand (John 2:20), and the disciples only understood after Jesus had risen from the dead (John 2:22). This is the background for Nicodemus coming to Jesus.

1) Nicodemus was wealthy. Jesus was usually surrounded by ordinary people, but Nicodemus must have been very wealthy. After the crucifixion of Jesus, Nicodemus brought "a mixture of myrrh and aloes about a hundred pound weight" (John 19:39). Only a wealthy man could have purchased that amount.

2) Nicodemus was a Pharisee. It is estimated there were only about 6,000 Pharisees. They vowed to spend all their lives observing the multitude of ceremonial laws. They had to be wealthy, in order to devote all their time to keeping the rules of Judaism. In order not to break any of the ten commandments, the Jews began to compile hundreds of laws to build a wall around them. The scribes were the principle authors of all the rules and regulations. For example the Bible simply states, "Remember the Sabbath day to keep it holy" and not to work on the Sabbath. The Mishnah is a Jewish book of scribal laws. There are twenty-four chapters devoted to Sabbath laws. The Talmud is the commentary on the Mishnah. The section on the Sabbath in the Talmud more than doubles the rules of the Mishnah. The scribes wrote the rules, and the Pharisees dedicated their lives to keep them. Nicodemus was a Pharisee, and it is amazing that he would want to talk to Jesus.

3) Nicodemus was a ruler of the Jews (John 3:1). That meant that he was a member of the Sanhedrin. The Sanhedrin had seventy members and was like the supreme court of the Jews. They had religious rule over all Jews everywhere. Again, it was amazing that Nicodemus should come to talk to Jesus.

4) Nicodemus came at night (John 3:2). This may have been a sign of caution. Perhaps he did not want other Pharisees or the Sanhedrin to know of his visit. It also could have been that this was the only time Nicodemus could have a private meeting with Jesus, since Jesus was usually surrounded by people all day.

THE ENCOUNTER

Nicodemus was impressed with the signs and wonders Jesus performed (John 3:2). He called Jesus "rabbi" and "teacher from God" (John 3:2). Jesus went straight to the heart of Nicodemus' problem. He needed to be born again (John 3:3). A man's life must be so changed that it could only be described as a new birth. Nicodemus misunderstood what Jesus meant.

The word translated "again" has three meanings. It can mean "from the beginning," "for the second time," or "from above." One English word cannot capture three meanings. All three meanings are involved. To be born again means to be radically changed from the way you began — such a radical change in a person's life, it is like being born for the second time, and the change is only possible by the grace and power of God.

Nicodemus responded, "How can I go into my mother's womb and be born again?" (John 3:4). He apparently believed that such a radical change was impossible.

If salvation were only for the elect or select few — as the Calvinists believe — why all the emphasis on being born again? Many New Testament passages talk about the new birth: 1 Peter 1:3, 22-23; James 1:18; Titus 3:5; Romans 6:1-11; 1 Corinthians 3:1-2; 2 Corinthians 5:17; Galatians 6:15; Ephesians 4:22-24; and Hebrews 5:12-14.

What does being "born again" mean for you? In John's gospel, there are four truths that are closely related to being "born again."

1) The kingdom of God (John 3:3): We must be born again to enter the kingdom of God. But what does the kingdom of God mean? In the

Lord's model prayer, He taught His disciples to pray: "Thy kingdom come, Thy will be done in earth as it is in heaven" (Matthew 6:10). When we are changed by the new birth, we enter into a relationship with God, in which our desire is to be submitted totally to the will of God.

2) The family of God (John 1:12): To those who believe, there is given the power to become His children. A sign of truly being a part of the family of God is obedience. "He that hath my commandments, and keepeth them, he it is that loveth Me" (John 14:21). Again, this involves accepting the will of God.

3) Eternal life (John 3:16): Eternal life is not just ordinary life only much longer. It is the kind of life that God possesses.

4) Believe (John 3:15): The only way a person will enter the kingdom of God is by believing in Jesus as Savior and Lord.

These four ideas are dependent upon our being born again. We are all sinners. We cannot accomplish this radical change on our own. Only the grace of God is able to cleanse us of our sin, change us and bring us into His kingdom. Only Jesus can work that change in us.

When that happens, we are born of water and the Spirit (John 3:5). Our physical birth is represented by water. The Spirit represents our second birth. When Jesus takes control of our lives, our past is forgotten and forgiven. But that's not all. Jesus' power at work in us enables us to have victory in the future.

When you are born again, you are changed. When you believe and love Jesus, He enters your life and dwells in you. Your past is forgiven and your future is secure.

You become a child of the King. You enter the kingdom of God. You have eternal life.

JESUS EXPLAINS GOD'S PLAN OF SALVATION (JOHN 3:7-21)

Nicodemus did not seem to understand what Jesus was saying. It is possible that this was a radical concept that was beyond Nicodemus' ability to understand. However, Jesus said to him: "Are you the teacher of Israel, and do not know these things?" (John 3:10). Apparently Nicodemus' problem was that he did not want to understand. He refused to see. His background as a Pharisee might have caused him to close his mind, because he did not want to change. If you do not want to change, you close your eyes, your mind, and your heart to the Lord who has the power to change you.

Jesus, in response to Nicodemus being unwilling to understand, said, "Do not marvel that I said to you, you must be born again" (John 3:7). Nicodemus should not have been surprised or amazed at what Jesus had said. He knew the Scriptures and should have remembered passages like Ezekiel 36:26: "A new heart I will give you, and a new spirit will I put within you." Jesus then told Nicodemus a mini parable in verse 8. The illustration involves the wind and the spirit. The Hebrew word for "spirit" is the same word for "wind." That is also true in the Greek language.

Jesus said: "You can hear and feel the wind, but you don't know where it comes from or where it is going." We don't know all about the wind, but the effects of the wind are plain to see. Jesus applied this illustration to the Spirit. We don't know how the Spirit works, but we can see the effects of the Spirit in our lives and the lives of others. Most of us know adults who have trusted Christ as Lord and Savior who have been radically changed. We may not understand the details of nuclear fusion, but we benefit from nuclear power plants that produce electricity.

NICODEMUS QUESTIONED JESUS' ANSWER (JOHN 3:9)

Nicodemus responded, "How does that work?" Jesus had tried to use simple examples from everyday life. As a teacher of Israel he should have understand (John 3:10). The problem was that Nicodemus did not receive Jesus' witness (John 3:11). If Nicodemus would not believe this earthly illustration, how would he even believe spiritual truth? (John 3:12). It is possible to intellectually understand the Christian faith, but not experience the power of the Holy Spirit. When you believe and commit your life to Jesus, you experience His presence. Jesus is the only one who can speak with authority, because He is the only one to descend from heaven. Jesus had come from the Father to reveal the Father and His truth (John 3:13).

Jesus then reminded Nicodemus of the event in Numbers 21:4-9. Israel was in the wilderness and began to murmur and complain about leaving Egypt. God sent a plague of serpents to punish them for their rebellion. The people repented. God then told Moses to make an image of a serpent and hold it up on a pole. The people were told they would be healed if they looked at the serpent. The people who believed and obeyed Moses were healed. They were not healed by the image of the serpent, but by believing in the Lord who commanded Moses to do this. Jesus applied this event to Himself. He would be lifted up on a cross and "whoever believes in Him should not perish, but have eternal life" (John 3:14-15).

Lift up

This word is used of Jesus in two ways. It is used of Jesus being "lifted up" on the cross (John 8:28; 12:32). The word is also used of Jesus being "lifted up" into glory (Acts 2:33). Jesus was lifted up on the cross and lifted up in the ascension. Jesus went willingly to the cross for us and ascended to glory in heaven. We have a choice. We can willingly take up our cross and follow Jesus, or refuse to do so. But if there is no cross, there is no crown.

The gospel in one verse (John 3:16)

1) "For God": This verse reveals that salvation began in the heart and mind of the Lord. Our God is not an angry, stern, unforgiving, legalistic god that must be appeased. This verse reveals that redeeming us was His idea.

2) *"... so loved":* "God is love" (1 John 4:8). God is our loving Father who desires for us to come to Him and respond to His love by loving Him. God's love is a selfless love. The Lord's love wants what is best for us. The Lord's love will dwell in believers (John 14:23).

3) *"... the world":* God's love encompasses the whole world — not just a certain nation, or good people, or people who love Him. All have the opportunity to enter into a love relationship with the Lord.

4) *"... that He gave His only begotten Son":* God's love is a giving love. There are givers and takers in this world. God is the Giver! He gave His only, unique Son to die for our sins.

5) *"... whoever believes in Him":* "Whoever" means anyone, anytime, anywhere can commit their heart and life to Jesus Christ . "Believe" means to trust and obey. A true disciple is one who follows the teachings and the lifestyle of Jesus.

6) *"... should not perish but have everlasting life":* Believers will not be consigned to an eternity in hell — a living death — but will possess the Father's kind of life, eternal and wonderful.

LOVE AND JUDGMENT

1) *The Father's purpose:* Jesus' purpose in coming to the world was for salvation, not condemnation (John 3:17).

2) *The result:* When a person is confronted with Jesus, he has a choice. If a person does not believe, he is condemned, because "he has not believed in the name of the only begotten Son of God" (John 3:18).

3) *The problem:* The problem is that some people love darkness. Their deeds are evil. They do not want to change ... they refuse to come to the light of the Lord Jesus (John 3:19). They are practicing evil. That

is their lifestyle. They refuse to come to the light (John 3:20).

4) *The truth:* Truth is not just something you say; truth is also what you do. Your deeds prove that you are following Jesus (John 3:21).

The Lord has created you with the ability to choose to respond to His gift of love. You can refuse and continue to live in the darkness. However, if you believe (trust and obey) Jesus, you will not perish, but have everlasting life.

The choice is in front of you. Will you choose life? Or by not choosing Jesus, you will have chosen death. Choose the love of the Lord Jesus and live in His love.

PERSON 2: THE SAMARITAN WOMAN (JOHN 4:1-26)

This powerful encounter between Jesus and the Samaritan woman is a very familiar Scripture passage to most of us. Jesus left Judea because He did not want to be drawn into a controversy about baptism with the Pharisees (John 4:1). The land of Palestine was divided into three sections: Galilee was in the North, Judea was in the South, and Samaria was in the middle. This land area was 120 miles from north to south.

When the Jews were traveling north or south, they traveled around Samaria on the other side of the Jordan River. This route took six days, whereas the direct route through Samaria took only three days. The reason for taking the longer route was due to the hostility between the Jews and the Samaritans. It all began when the Northern Kingdom was conquered by the Assyrians in 720 BC. The Assyrians moved other conquered people in and moved many of the inhabitants out. Because of intermarriage, they were considered by the Jews as totally corrupt. When the Jews returned to Jerusalem from the Babylonian captivity in 450 BC, the Samaritans offered to help rebuild the temple, but they were rejected by the Jews. So the Samaritans build a temple on Mt. Gerizim.

The Jews had no dealings with the Samaritans (John 4:9). They would not ever allow the shadow of a Samaritan to fall across their shadow. Yet Jesus "needed to go through Samaria" (John 4:4).

JESUS BROKE DOWN THE WALLS

1) The barrier between the Jews and Samaritans had been there for 400 years. Yet Jesus traveled through Samaria. Jesus stopped at Jacob's well near the city of Sychar. Jesus was "weary from His journey" (John 4:5-6). This demonstrated Jesus' humanity. The disciples went on to the city to buy food (John 4:8). Prior to following Jesus, the disciples would not have entered Samaria or gone to a Samaritan village to purchase food.

2) The barrier between men and women was well defined in their culture. Rabbis were forbidden to speak to a woman in public, not even their wife or sister. It was about the sixth hour (noon), and a Samaritan woman came to draw water from the well. Jesus asked her for a drink (John 4:6-7). Jesus not only spoke to a woman, she was a Samaritan and a woman of corrupt character. The village women would have come together early in the morning to draw water for cooking and drinking for the day. She came in the middle of the day by herself. She was rejected by the other women in the village. Jesus asked her for a drink, and her response was a question. She seemed to be shocked, and surprised. Her question revealed her prejudice against the Jews: "How is it that You, being a Jew, ask a drink from me, a Samaritan woman?" (John 4:9).

JESUS OFFERED HER LIVING WATER

1) Jesus' response is very revealing. Jesus said, "If you knew" three times (John 4:10): If you knew the gift of God; if you knew who is speaking to you; if you knew who said give Me a drink, you would have asked Him, and He would have given you living water. Jesus' implication was that she did not know. The "who" she was speaking to was the Lord, who had a gift from God for her — and if she knew He was the King of kings, she would have asked for living water.

"Living water" referred to flowing water, in contrast to a pond or pool or a well. Of course, she did not know who Jesus was and took Jesus literally. Notice her answer. "You have nothing to draw with, and the well is deep. Where then will you get that living water?" (John 4:11). Jesus had no bucket for water. The well was 100 feet deep, and water seeped into the well through the ground. It was not flowing water. There was no flowing water anywhere near where they were. She then asked, "Are you greater than our father Jacob, who gave us this well?"(John 4:12). She thought what Jesus said was impossible.

Jesus then made it clear. The kind of "water" Jesus offered was for a thirsty soul, and if she received it she would never thirst again. It would be a fountain of water that would bring eternal life (John 4:13-14). This fountain of life keeps flowing within you when you become a believer.

Have you ever seen an artesian spring? I have seen one on the Cumberland Plateau. In the 1920s, a group built a dam to contain a small lake for swimming from the flow of water from the artesian spring, and built resort housing. The development was called "Waldensia." This woman responded to Jesus in a sarcastic, joking way. "Give that water to me so I won't be thirsty and won't have to ever draw water again" (John 4:15). The woman was blind because she refused to see. Jesus had made a Messianic claim: "They shall not hunger or thirst" (Isaiah 49:10), and "With Thee is the fountain of life" (Psalm 36:9). She refused to see and believe.

THE WOMAN HAD TO FACE THE TRUTH

Jesus brought this woman to face the truth of her situation by telling her to go and bring back her husband (John 4:16). She admitted she had no husband (John 4:17). Jesus responded that she told the truth.

She was living with a man and they were not married, and she had five husbands before him (John 4:17-18). Jesus revealed her sin.

The woman had her first glimmer of recognition and responded, "You are a prophet" (John 4:19). Thinking Jesus a prophet, she brought up a religious question. Who is right? We worship here on this mountain and you Jews worship in Jerusalem (John 4:20). She was asking, "Where can I find God?"

1) Jesus began His answer with the truth that worship of the Lord is not a matter of a specific place (John 4:21).

2) Jesus stated that Israel had a unique place in God's plan of salvation. God called them to be a nation of faith in Him and witnesses to the world. The Redeemer came through Israel (John 4:22).

3) True worship is not a matter of form, style, or tradition: for "God is Spirit, and those who worship Him, must worship in spirit and truth" (John 4:23).

This was all new to her. It was beyond her understanding. She knew the Messiah was coming, and she believed He could explain everything (John 4:25). Jesus responded, "I ... am He" (John 4:26). In this woman's encounter with Jesus, she heard the greatest truth ever expressed: Jesus is the Christ!

This woman's story began when she was a hated, rejected Samaritan, and in her time a lonely woman in society, a woman living in sin — but then she met Jesus. Jesus revealed to her that He was the Messiah.

The woman went from thinking of Jesus just as a Jewish man, to a prophet, and perhaps the Messiah.

Have you faced your life? Have you been honest with yourself? Will you confess your sin? Will you believe that Jesus is the Christ, the Son of God?

THE HARVEST (JOHN 4:27-45)

THE DISCIPLES

When the disciples returned they were amazed that Jesus was talking to a woman. The Jewish rabbis thought that women were not able to understand any deep teaching about religious things. By rabbinic rules, Jesus could not have done anything more radical than talking with a Samaritan woman. However, the disciples had been with Jesus long enough that they did not question His actions. In order to follow Jesus, they were learning to drop their prejudices and their Jewish customs.

THE SAMARITAN WOMAN

In the meantime, the woman left to go back to her village (John 4:28). She was so much in a hurry to share her discovery of the Messiah that she left her water jar. She was so convicted about whom she had been talking with, she forgot the reason she had gone to the well! She was convicted by two things: (1) She was amazed that Jesus knew all about her (John 4:29). Psalm 139:1-4, "O Lord, You have searched me and known me. You know my sitting down and my rising up; You understand my thought afar off. You comprehend my path and my lying down and are acquainted with all my ways. For there is not a word on my tongue, But behold, O Lord, You know it altogether." (2) The Samaritan woman was also awakening to the possibility that Jesus was the Messiah (John 4:29).

Being convicted of these two powerful truths, her first thought was to tell others. Our Christian life should be marked by our desire to tell others about Jesus. Over forty-three years ago, the Lord led me to the truth that the two main focuses of our Christian faith are: To know Christ, and to make Him known. This truth was the guiding principle I shared with the last three churches I have pastored. It is a great, brief purpose statement that emphasizes the essential elements of our faith. The Samaritan woman realized this truth immediately. She came to know Christ and her first impulse was to tell others. She was so energized to tell the villagers about Jesus that she forgot about being an outcast.

If you were saved as an adult, you can testify to others about how your life was changed when you trusted Jesus as your Lord and Savior. I want to challenge you to write out your testimony in 100 words or less. The outline for your testimony is to write briefly what your life was like before you met Jesus. Then state the fact that you trusted Jesus as your Lord and Savior. The third step is to briefly tell how Jesus has changed your life. During this coronavirus crisis, you have the time to think about your testimony and briefly put your thoughts on paper.

The woman's testimony was effective because the people were moved to go out and meet Jesus (John 4:30).

THE DISCIPLES

"In the meantime His disciples urged Him, saying, 'Rabbi, eat'" (John 4:31). When the disciples had left Jesus, He was tired and hungry. But now Jesus ignored the food. So the disciples urged Him to eat. Jesus replied that He had other food to eat (John 4:32). The disciples misunderstood and reasoned that someone else had given Him food (John 4:33). Jesus' response revealed His purpose for coming to earth: "My food is to do the will of Him who sent Me" (John 4:34). Jesus' heart was to obey His Heavenly Father. John's gospel uses two different Greek words that can be translated "sent." John used one word seven times, and he used the other word twenty-seven. So forty-four times, John pointed out that Jesus was sent by His Father. "I came down from heaven not to do my own will, but the will of Him who sent Me" (John 6:38).

Teaching Opportunity

Jesus always seized the moment in order to drive home the meaning of events. There was a common saying: "There are still four months and then comes the harvest" (John 4:35). Normally from the time of the sowing of the seed, it took four months until harvest time. Then Jesus declared: "Behold ... lift up your eyes ... look ... the fields are white for harvest" (John 4:35). Wake up! The harvest is now. This is the spiritual harvest that leads to eternal life (John 4:36). There is such a short time between sowing and harvesting that sower and harvester can rejoice together (John 4:36). Here in Samaria, Jesus sowed seed and the harvest was ready. The disciples did not sow, but they could participate in the harvest (John 4:37).

Jesus' greatest "sowing" was on the cross. In dying for our sin He was buried as a seed in the earth (John 12:24). In Jesus' resurrection, He was the first fruits of a great harvest of souls that would follow (1 Corinthians 15:20, 23). "But now Christ is risen from the dead, and has become the first fruits .... But each one in his own order: Christ the first fruit, afterward those who are Christ's at His coming." Disciples, then and now, are challenged to enter into the harvest for the Lord.

The Samaritans

Notice that "many of the Samaritans believed on Him" (John 4:39). Their faith rested on three things:

1) The testimony of the woman about Jesus and His power to know all about her (John 4:39). We, too, can introduce people to Jesus. What a privilege!

2) They had a desire to know for themselves. To come to a personal decision about Jesus, the Samaritans needed to know Jesus better. So they invited Jesus to stay. Jesus stayed two days with them (John 4:40). People need to hear the gospel, but they must come to the point of faith for themselves. We can't be saved for someone else. Your parent's faith won't save you. You must believe for yourselves.

3) Finally, the Samaritans believed for themselves (John 4:41). They told the woman: "Now we believe not because of what you said, for we ourselves have heard Him and we know that this is, indeed, the Christ, the Savior of the world" (John 4:42).

The Samaritan woman is an example of the saving, transforming power of the Lord Jesus Christ, the Savior of the world. I'm sure she would have been the first to admit that she was living a sinful life. When Jesus came, Jesus enabled her to break away from the past and be changed. She now had a whole new future. Jesus had explained the new birth to Nicodemus in Chapter 3, and here in Chapter 4 the new birth was a reality for the Samaritan woman. Salvation is open to anyone in the world (John 4:42). Jesus' saving grace is available to you today. Will you admit your sin and come to Jesus and discover new life? Your future will be certain when you put your future in the hands of your Savior, the Lord Jesus Christ.

PERSON 3: THE NOBLEMAN (JOHN 4:46-54)

Right after John recorded Jesus' encounter with a sinful woman from hated Samaria, he related the encounter of Jesus with an official from King Herod's court.

Jesus returned to Cana in Galilee. John reminded his readers that this was the village where Jesus did His first sign, turning water into wine (John 4:46). When we studied the seven signs described in John's gospel, this encounter with the nobleman was the second sign (John 4:54).

THE NOBLEMAN

The word translated "nobleman" (John 4:46) was a word used for a royal official, a member of a king's court. Today, it would be like being a member of the president's cabinet. Nicodemus was a high Jewish official, a member of the Sanhedrin. The Nobleman was a high Roman government official, a member of King Herod's court. John gave witness to the truth that all people need Jesus — the "up and ins" and the "down and outs."

HUMILITY

What would it take for you to humble yourself and admit to the Lord and others that you are a sinner in need of grace and forgiveness? What would it take for you to publicly acknowledge faith in the Lord Jesus, be baptized and join the church? You would have to swallow your pride and not care what your friends or others thought. Only the humble will come to Jesus. Only the humble can come to Jesus! The nobleman humbled himself.

The nobleman loved his son. He loved his son so much he was willing to travel the twenty miles from Capernaum to Cana (John 4:46). He loved his son so much he was willing to beg a common carpenter-preacher to heal his son (John 4:47). He loved his son so much he did not care what his fellow government officials thought. He loved his son so much he was not deterred by what his family, friends, or neighbors thought. The nobleman had probably exhausted every other possibility of a cure.

DETERMINATION

The nobleman was determined to do whatever it took for his son to be healed. Jesus said: "Unless you people see signs and wonders, you will by no means believe" (John 4:48). There was apparently a crowd around Jesus. They would have been curious to see what Jesus would do.

Perhaps Jesus was aiming this comment for all to hear. The important question that Jesus wanted them and us to answer is, "Do you believe that Jesus is the Son of God, the Messiah?" No matter what miracles Jesus did, many religious leaders wanted more proof. The problem was not a lack of proof, but a lack of faith. Jesus was looking for faith in the lives of those He encountered.

The nobleman begged Jesus "to come before my child dies" (John 4:49). Jesus apparently sensed the father's faith and responded, "Go your way, your son lives." Notice the man's response, "So the man believed the word that Jesus spoke to him, and he went his way" (John 4:50).

The problem today with so many who say they are Christians or say they are church members is that they do not live like they believe Jesus' word. Some want a god created in their image, a god that does what they want and approves what they do. Some only accept that part of God's Word that appeals to them or that won't interfere with their worldly lifestyle.

Faith

The father believed Jesus and started back to Capernaum. On his way, his servant met him and told him, "Your son lives" (John 4:51). After asking the servants when his son was made well, he realized it was the same time when Jesus had said, "Your son lives" (John 4:52-53). This was such an incredible miracle that not only the nobleman, but his whole household were saved (John 4:53).

It is vital that we do not just give lip service to the Lord, but truly believe and obey Jesus. That means being committed to do what Jesus has said in His Word: the Bible.

Imagine how difficult it would be today for a well-known high public official to go public with his faith in Jesus. They might be concerned about how other government officials would react, or how the media would media report it. Or how would the voting public respond to his newfound faith?

The nobleman faced these circumstances because of his radical decision to believe in Jesus. Have you made the radical decision to follow Jesus no matter what family, friends, and fellow workers might say?

As Joshua declared in front of the leaders Israel and all the tribes gathered at Shechem: "Choose for yourselves this day whom you will serve … . But as for me and my house, we will serve the Lord." (Joshua 24:15). Now it is one thing to say, "I will serve the Lord," and it is another to actually do it. James wrote: "Be doers of the word, and not hearers only, deceiving yourselves" (James 1:22). We deceive ourselves if all we do is hear the word and then do not do it. When I was a boy and failed to do what my mother told me to do, she would say, "What I tell you goes in one ear and out the other!" How many sermons have you heard in your lifetime? How many Bible study lessons have you heard? It does not benefit you at all if you have heard thousands, and do not obey the Word you have heard. James also declared: "Thus also faith by itself, if it does not have works, is dead" (James 2:17).

The noun "faith" came from the verb "to believe." A verb is an action word. So faith is something you do. "To believe" means "to trust and obey." Becoming a Christian is more than saying a few words. It is a matter of repentance, a change of mind, a change of heart, and a change of behavior.

Have you come to the point in your life where you are determined to love Jesus and live for Jesus?

Person 4: The Lame Man (John 5:1-30)

The fourth person to encounter Jesus was a poor, helpless, and hopeless man. John had related the encounters with Nicodemus, a wealthy Pharisee and member of the Sanhedrin; a sinful Samaritan woman; a wealthy nobleman in Herod's court; and now a man lame for thirty-eight years (John 5:5).

THE LAME MAN

We have looked at this man's story as John's third sign that Jesus was the Son of God. Briefly then, Jesus was in Jerusalem to observe one of the feasts of Israel (John 5:1). Jesus went to the pool of Bethesda, which means "house of mercy" (John 5:2). Sick people gathered there with the hope of being healed (John 5:3). The Jews believed that the first person in the water, when it was stirred, would be healed (John 5:4). One desperate person had been lame for thirty-eighty years (John 5:5). Jesus approached him and asked him, "Do you want to be made well?" (John 5:6). His reply indicated "yes," but he had no one to help him into the water (John 5:7). Jesus commanded him to take up his pallet and walk (John 5:8). Immediately the man was healed, but it was the Sabbath (John 5:9).

When Jesus healed this lame man on the Sabbath, it set off a firestorm among the Jews (John 5:10). The Jews questioned the man about carrying a burden on the Sabbath, and he told them a man told him to do it (John 5:11-13). Carrying a burden on the Sabbath was punishable by stoning the offender to death. Later, Jesus met the man in the temple and told him to sin no more (John 5:14). The man then told the Jews it was Jesus who had healed him (John 5:15). The man had been cured of an impossible condition, and this should have been a time of rejoicing. But the legalistic Jews only saw this as breaking their laws. The Jews had thousands of little rules. The rabbis even said it was a sin if you carried a needle in your garment on the Sabbath! The Jews used this event to persecute Jesus, and "they sought to kill Him" (John 5:16).

Jesus' Response

This passage is one of the long discourses of Jesus in John's gospel. And it is amazing because every one of those statements of Jesus is a clear claim that He is the promised Messiah. The Jews would have clearly understood what Jesus was saying. It was really a question of acceptance. Would they accept Jesus' claims or not?

1) Jesus clearly stated that He had equality with God His Father. They both were always working (John 5:17). The Jews were further angered because they understood that Jesus was claiming God was His Father, making Himself equal to God (John 5:18).

2) Jesus clearly stated that He was doing exactly what His Father was doing (John 5:19). Jesus was following the mind and heart of the Lord God. The Jews' eyes were on their rules and not on the ways of the Lord.

3) Jesus clearly stated that the Father loves the Son and reveals to Him what His Father is doing (John 5:20). The Greek word *agape* is always used of God's love in the New Testament. It is a selfless love that always wants what is best for others. There are two words for God's love in the Old Testament: *hen* and *hesed*. Usually they are not translated with one word, but by a combination like "everlasting love" or "lovingkindness." This is the bond of love between the Father and the Son. And it is the bond of love that Jesus wants to give us.

4) Jesus clearly stated that the Father raises the dead, and the Son can do this also (John 5:21). The Jews knew that the Old Testament stated that only God would raise the dead (Deuteronomy 32:39). But Jesus would raise Lazarus from the dead! The Jewish leaders had so hardened their hearts that even the raising of Lazarus did not convince them (John 12:10).

5) Jesus clearly stated that the Father has committed judgment to His Son (John 5:22). Again, judgment was solely God's prerogative. If

KEN CLAYTON   97

they believed that Jesus had the right to judge, they were obligated to listen to Him and obey Him.

6) *Jesus clearly stated* that He is to receive the same honor as the Father. If they do not honor the Son, they are not honoring the Father (John 5:23). They thought their religion honored God, but they were rejecting Jesus. To reject Jesus was to reject God.

7) *Jesus clearly stated* that anyone who hears and believes His word has everlasting life and will not be judged, but "has passed from death to life" (John 5:24).

8) *Jesus clearly stated* that the resurrection is coming, and that both the Son of God and the Father give life (John 5:25-26, 28-29). The "hour" was like a code word for God's appointed time for the revelation of His Son and His plan of salvation. Those already dead will hear Jesus' voice and be resurrected. Some will be resurrected to life, and some to condemnation. As Jesus said, "I am the resurrection and the life. He who believes in Me, though he may die, he shall live" (John 11:25).

9) *Jesus clearly stated* that God had given Him the authority to judge, because Jesus had come as the Son of Man (John 5:27). The phrase, "Son of man," was in Daniel 7:1-14. Daniel had a vision of the glory that would come some day. Daniel described the great heathen empires as beasts. The Babylonian Empire was a lion; the Median Empire was a bear; the Persian Empire a leopard, and the Greek Empire a beast with iron teeth and ten horns. But one day would come a power that will be kind, gracious, and gentle. It will be led by a man, not a beast. This new age would be ushered in by the Messiah, the "Son of Man." So when Jesus called Himself "Son of Man," He was calling Himself the Messiah.

10) *Jesus clearly stated* that He was not doing His will, but the will of the Father who sent Him (John 5:30). "And this is the will of Him who sent Me, that everyone who sees the Son and believes in Him may have everlasting life; and I will raise him up at the last day" (John 6:40).

The Old Testament pointed to the fact that Messiah would be the fulfillment of all of these things. However the Jews built their religion on their legalistic rules that really had no place for the Messiah.

Jesus clearly claimed rights that belonged to God alone. Jesus claimed powers and functions that belonged to the Messiah. This sounded like blasphemy to the Jews. Jesus claimed to be the King. So those listening were faced with a choice: either to accept Jesus as the Son of God, or hate Him as a blasphemer and destroy Him. You, too, are faced with a choice. You must either accept Jesus as King of kings and Lord of lords, or you reject His claim and destroy yourself.

Person 5: The Woman Caught in Adultery (John 8:1-11)

The fifth person John recorded, that Jesus encountered, was a woman caught in the act of adultery. Before we focus on this unusual encounter, we need to look at the circumstances that led up to this extreme trap that the scribes and Pharisees sprang on Jesus.

It is important in approaching any passage of Scripture to recognize the context leading up to the event. The seventh chapter of John is filled with examples of the growing hostility of the Jewish leaders and their plotting to trap Jesus.

The Background

In scanning through Chapter 7, notice that it was the time for the Feast of Tabernacles (John 7:2). The chapter begins with criticism from Jesus' brothers, who as yet did not believe in Him (John 7:3-5). There are many examples of hostility in Chapter 7: "… much complaining among the people concerning Him. … He deceives the people" (John 7:12); "How does this Man know letters, having never studied?" (John 7:15); "You have a demon. Who is seeking to kill you?" (John 7:20);

"Now some of them from Jerusalem said, 'Is this not He whom they seek to kill?'"(John 7:25); "However, we know where this Man is from; but when the Christ comes, no one knows where He is from" (John 7:27); "Therefore they sought to take Him; but no one laid a hand on Him, because His hour had not yet come" (John 7:30); "The Pharisees heard the crowd murmuring these things concerning Him, and the Pharisees and the chief priests sent officers to take Him" (John 7:32); "So there was a division among the people because of Him" (John 7:43); when the officers reported back to the chief priests and the Pharisees that they had not arrested Jesus, they stated, "No man ever spoke like this man!" (John 7:46); "Are you also deceived?" (John 7:47); "But this crowd that does not know the law is accursed" (John 7:49); One of them, Nicodemus, said, "Does our law judge a man before it hears him and knows what he is doing?" (John 7:50-51).

THE PLOT

Now the stage is set for this elaborate plot to trap Jesus. Chapter 8 begins with Jesus going to the temple early, and people gathered around Him and He taught them.

Jesus' teaching was interrupted when the scribes and Pharisees brought a woman caught in the very act of adultery (John 8:4). Moses in the law commanded the death penalty. What do you say? (John 8:5).

The scribes and Pharisees were trying to find a charge against Jesus that would justify them in their plot to destroy Jesus. Somehow they managed to catch this woman in the act of committing adultery. Had they been spying and waiting for such an opportunity? We don't know. In Leviticus 20:10, it states that "adulterer and adulteress shall be put to death." Where was the man? They were not so much concerned with the law as they were with trapping Jesus. They were using her. She was just a thing. It is doubtful that they even knew her name.

Have you ever noticed the importance of names in the Bible? There are whole pages of lists of who begot who! Even the New Testament begins with a list of names in Jesus' family line (Matthew 1:1-17). Names had meaning. For example: Jacob, the "deceiver," became "Israel," or "prince with God" (Genesis 32:28). The Bible is not the story of unnamed masses of people, but of individuals that tell the story of God working in their lives, moving history to His conclusion. We are not things in the eyes of God. He knows you by name. Jesus died on the cross for you.

THE DILEMMA

If Jesus said simply, "Stone her," the common people might think Jesus was harsh. The people had been drawn to Jesus because of His loving, caring, healing ministry. Also, Jesus would have been at odds with the Roman authorities, because they were the only ones who had the authority to execute anyone. Now, if Jesus had simply pardoned her, He would have broken the law of Moses. The Jews would have accused Jesus of condoning adultery. The Jews thought they had trapped Jesus: "This they said, testing Him ..." (John 8:6a).

JESUS COUNTERED THEIR ATTACK

"But Jesus stooped down and wrote on the ground with His finger ..." (John 8:6b). What was Jesus doing? The Scriptures do not tell us. There are a few possibilities:

1) Perhaps Jesus was giving them time to realize how deceitful they were.

2) Perhaps Jesus was giving them time to realize how cruelly they were using this woman.

3) But it seems to me the best explanation is that Jesus was writing in the dirt the sins of her accusers. The common Greek word for "write" is not used here. A compound Greek word is used that means "to write down a record against someone." For example in Job 13:26, "For you write bitter things against me." So Jesus may have been confronting these men with a list of their own sins.

JESUS RESPONDED

They continued asking Him, so Jesus raised up and said: "He who is without sin among you, let him throw a stone at her first" (John 8:7). Jesus then returned to writing on the ground (John 8:8). There was silence. Then the men drifted away, beginning with the oldest. Jesus' answer revealed that only a sinless person had the right to judge. "Judge not, that you be not judged" (Matthew 7:1). Now since "we all have sinned and come short of the glory of God" (Romans 3:23), only the Lord has the right to judge. Jesus is holy and without sin. You and I do not qualify as judges of others.

Jesus' earthly life revealed His deep compassion for others. In Matthew 9:36: "But when He saw the multitudes, He was moved with compassion for them, because they were weary and scattered, like sheep having no shepherd." As followers of Jesus, our first reaction toward others should be compassion. Jesus had compassion for this woman.

JESUS' CONVERSATION WITH THE WOMAN

When the men had left, Jesus raised up and asked, "Where are those accusers of yours? Has no one condemned you?" (John 8:10). Note her answer, "No one, Lord" (John 8:11). She called Jesus "Lord." In those moments in Jesus' presence, she must have sensed who He was. Jesus responded: "Neither do I condemn you; go and sin no more" (John 8:11). Jesus did not condone her sin or simply give her a free pass. Jesus gave her a second chance. When we come to Jesus in true repentance of our sins, He forgives us. "If we confess our sins, He is faithful and just to forgive us our sins and to cleanse us from all unrighteousness" (1 John 1:9). Jesus gave her a challenge: "Go and sin no more" (John 8:11). Her life had to demonstrate that she had repented, been changed, and had begun a new life.

When our children, Jill and Kenny, were young, they enjoyed playing miniature golf. When they would putt the golf ball and it went off course, they would say, "Do over!" We would let them run, pick up the ball and putt again. Jesus really gives us a "do over" for life. When we come to Jesus in faith, our lives are changed, and our goal is to "sin no more."

With the Holy Spirit dwelling in each believer, we are able to live a life that can be more and more like the person the Lord wants us to become.

What happened to this woman? We don't know. Her story is unfinished in the Scripture. But since John included the encounter of Jesus and this woman, it is quite possible that she truly believed and was a remembered person in the early church.

What will happen with you? Your story is unfinished too. My desire is to be able to say with Paul: "I have fought the good fight, I have finished the race, I have kept the faith" (2 Timothy 4:7). How about you?

Person 6: The Man Born Blind (John 9:35-41)

We have focused our attention on this passage earlier, when Jesus gave sight to the man born blind. John pointed to this as the sixth sign that Jesus is the Son of God. Although blindness was common in Jesus' day, being born blind was especially tragic. There was no cure for one born blind.

The Jews believed there was a connection between sin and suffering. They believed that sin caused this man's blindness. They believed that this man had sinned, or his parents had sinned, to cause the blindness (John 9:1-2). Jesus responded to the disciples question by saying, "Neither, but that the works of God be revealed in him" (John 9:3).

Then Jesus spat on the ground and made a clay paste and put it on the man's eyes (John 9:6). Jesus commanded the man to go to the Pool of Siloam and wash his eyes. The man obeyed, and he was healed (John 9:7).

The man was then questioned by neighbors and the Pharisees (John 9:13-14). Also, the Pharisees questioned the man's parents (John 9:18-23). When the man would not denounce Jesus or change his testimony about his healing, the Pharisees became very angry (John 9:24-34). So the Pharisees "cast him out" (John 9:34). That meant he was excluded from synagogue and temple worship, and from the life of Israel.

Jesus found the man and revealed to him that He was the Son of God (John 9:38). This powerful healing encounter was a sign that proved Jesus was the Son of God. Jesus' encounter with the man born blind also revealed some wonderful truths about Jesus.

1) The absolute power to heal: Jesus demonstrated His healing power to overcome a most difficult disease, blindness from birth. "Nothing is impossible with God" (Luke 1:37). During these difficult times of the worldwide pandemic, we know that the Lord has the power to heal. The Lord has promised believers: "I will never leave you nor forsake you" (Hebrews 13:5). The word "never" is the most empathetic "no" in Greek. It is like saying "never" seven times! Our Lord Jesus is going before us, is with us now, and will bring us to our heavenly home one day.

2) Jesus seized every opportunity to serve the Father (John 9:4). Jesus did not waste time. He was aware of the work the Father had commissioned Him to do. You and I must seize the moment. We must use every opportunity to reflect the love, mercy, and power of the Lord upon our lost world.

3) Jesus used this encounter to declare who He is. Jesus said: "I am [Who I Am] the light of the world" (John 9:5). Jesus claimed the personal name that God had revealed to Moses in the burning bush — "I Am Who I Am." Jesus stated that He is the God of light for all people everywhere. Only Jesus can illuminate our problems, our situation, our needs, our hopes, and our fears. Psalm 27:1 declares: "The Lord is my light and my salvation; whom shall I fear?" John later wrote: "This is the message which we have heard from Him and declare to you, that God is light and in Him is no darkness at all" (1 John 1:5). "But if we walk in the light as He is in the light, we have fellowship with one another, and the blood of Jesus Christ His Son cleanses us from all sin" (1 John 1:7).

4) Jesus came to seek and save the lost (Luke 19:10). Jesus declared that seeking and saving the lost was a priority for Him. So after the Pharisees had questioned the man born blind, and had been unable to force him to denounce Jesus or change his healing testimony, they excommunicated him. That meant he was ostracized from the community and from public worship (John 9:34).

Jesus then did what He said He would do. When Jesus heard the Pharisees had cast the man out, Jesus sought the man and found him (John 9:35). Jesus' main goal was the man's salvation, so Jesus asked, "Do you believe in the Son of God?" (John 9:35). The man expressed a desire to believe, but he did not know who the Son of God was (John 9:36). Basically Jesus said: "I Am" (John 9:37). The man cried out "Lord, I believe!" and he worshipped Jesus.

Jesus is still the seeking shepherd, looking for lost sheep. Jesus said, "I am the good shepherd. The good shepherd gives His life for the sheep" (John 10:11). Luke records this parable: "What man of you having one hundred sheep, if he loses one of them, does not leave the ninety-nine in the wilderness, and go after the one which is lost until he finds it? And when he has found it, he lays it on his shoulders, rejoicing. And when he comes home, he calls together his friends and neighbors, saying to them, 'Rejoice with me, for I have found my sheep which was lost!' I say to you that likewise there will be more joy in heaven over one sinner who repents than over ninety-nine just persons who need no repentance" (Luke 15:4-7).

We can plainly see the loving heart of Jesus portrayed in this self-portrait parable. Jesus is the loving, seeking Shepherd. Jesus sought out the man He had healed and confronted him with the opportunity to trust and obey Jesus as the Son of God.

JESUS IS THE JUDGE

In verse 39, Jesus said: "For judgment I have come into this world, that those who do not see may see, and that those who see may be made blind." Jesus' presence forced people to make a choice. If people chose to reject Jesus, they are pronouncing judgment upon themselves. "My judgment is righteousness, because I do not seek My own will but the will of the Father who sent Me" (John 5:30). In John 5:22, "For the Father judges no one, but has committed all judgment to the Son." There will come a time of judgment. However, Jesus' priority is salvation. John quoted Jesus saying in John 12:47: "And if anyone hears My words and does not believe, I do not judge him; for I did not come to judge the world but to save the world."

The encounter between Jesus and the man born blind highlighted these essential truths about Jesus.

As believers following the Lord Jesus Christ, we should exhibit these qualities in our lives. Jesus had absolute power to heal. We, too, should be seeking to heal broken relationships; to heal the wounded hearts of the lonely, dismayed or ignored people we know; to heal broken hearts;

and to bring ultimate healing for the soul by testifying to the saving power of Jesus.

Just as Jesus seized every opportunity to serve His Father, that should be our heart also. We should use our contacts with others to make sure they know who we are in Jesus. Our words and our lifestyle should declare that we belong to Jesus. Our goal should be the same as Jesus, to seek and save the lost.

Are you just a casual follower of Jesus, or are you a committed follower of Jesus? Examine your time schedule and your bank account. Check your priorities. Is your lifestyle equal to your words about your faith? In these difficult times, if you stand up for Jesus, you will stand out!

PERSON 7: LAZARUS (JOHN 11)

The seventh person that John recorded who Jesus encountered was Lazarus. This is one of the most powerful and revealing encounters in the Bible. We have studied this passage before because it was the seventh sign that John gave, which proved that Jesus was the Son of God. There are many highlights that are very revealing in the eleventh chapter of John.

PERSONAL RELATIONSHIPS

In the small village of Bethany, about two miles east of Jerusalem, was the house of Mary, Martha and Lazarus. Their friendship with Jesus was so strong that their home seemed to be Jesus' headquarters when He was in Jerusalem. When Lazarus became ill, the sisters sent word to Jesus, saying: "Lord, behold, he whom You love is sick" (John 11:3).

During these days of "stay at home" orders and quarantines due to the coronavirus, "home" becomes so much more important to most

Americans. It means more time for families to be together, to learn to work, play and live every day under one roof. It is an opportunity to grow closer, to learn to work together, and to realize the important principles of God's Word. Things like love, mercy, forgiveness, kindness and a servant's heart become real, or else home life can deteriorate into chaos.

Home should be a place where you can find love, peace, understanding and rest. Jesus found that in the house of Mary, Martha and Lazarus, who called Jesus "Lord" (John 11:3).

THE DELAY

The shock of this encounter is that, in spite of their close relationship, Jesus delayed His journey to Bethany for two days (John 11:6). Jesus had told the disciples that this had happened according to God's plan to glorify God and glorify God's Son (John 11:4).

It is clear in John's gospel that Jesus regarded the cross as His greatest glory. Jesus knew that bringing Lazarus back to life would glorify Him, but it would also mean taking a giant step that would lead directly to the cross.

Jesus departed for Bethany on His own schedule. Jesus is always on time, every time. We can trust Jesus to keep His promises. Jesus announced, "Let us go to Judea again" (John 11:7).

A TEACHABLE MOMENT

The disciples were aware of the hostility of the Jews. The Jews had even sought to stone Jesus (John 11:8). Jesus explained that while we have the light, we need to work in the light. A person stumbles when they do not have the light (John 11:9-10). Jesus knew God's timing. He knew God's opportunity. Jesus was working in the light. Jesus knew what He was going to do. And He knew this would strengthen their faith (John 11:15).

We must serve the Lord while we have the opportunity. We must focus our energy, time and resources to serve the Lord and bless other people in Jesus' name.

RESURRECTION AND LIFE

When Jesus arrived in Bethany, Lazarus had been in the tomb for four days (John 11:17). Jews did not mummify bodies like the Egyptians did. Bodies were wrapped in linen clothes with spices and laid in a tomb. There were many mourners comforting the sisters when Jesus arrived (John 11:19). Martha was upset that Jesus had come too late to save her brother (John 11:21). She followed that with a statement of faith: "I know that whatever You ask of God, God will give You" (John 11:22). As Jesus and Martha discussed the idea of the resurrection, Jesus revealed a powerful truth to Martha: "I am [Who I Am] the resurrection and the life. He who believes in Me, though he may die, he shall live" (John 11:25-26). Jesus used the personal name that God gave to Moses from the burning bush (Exodus 3:14). Jesus clearly claimed to be the Lord God Almighty present in this world. Jesus also claimed to be the resurrection. Jesus is the only One who has conquered death and hell. He was ready to prove this by raising Lazarus from the dead. The ultimate proof was His own resurrection after being crucified to pay the penalty for our sin. Jesus also claimed to be life. Jesus is the creator. "All things were made through Him, and without Him nothing was made that was made" (John 1:3). Jesus not only created life, He is the giver of eternal life (John 11:25-26).

MARTHA'S CONFESSION OF FAITH

Martha declared, "Yes, Lord, I believe that You are the Christ, the Son of God, who is to come into the world" (John 11:27). She called

Jesus "Lord." The first confession of faith is to say and believe "Jesus is Lord." Martha believed that Jesus was the Messiah, God's promised Anointed One, the Son of God! Have you believed in Jesus as Lord of your life? Have you honestly made a commitment to obey Jesus as your Lord and Savior?

Jesus approached the tomb and commanded that the stone be removed (John 11:39). Jesus spoke, and Lazarus came forth from the tomb (John 11:43). What should have been a joyous celebration for everyone was marred by the reaction of the Jewish leaders.

REACTION OF THE JEWS

Although some of the Jews believed in Jesus, others reported the event to the Pharisees (John 11:45-46). The chief priests and the Pharisees called a meeting of the Sanhedrin to decide what to do. Jesus' powerful "signs" were convincing people that He was the Messiah (John 11:47). The Sadducees were afraid "everyone will believe in Him," and the Romans would come and take away their place and nation (John 11:48). The leading Jews had collaborated with the Romans, and the Romans allowed them to rule. The Jewish leaders thought more of their system of power and wealth than they did their relationship with God. How about you? Are your finances or position more important to you than obeying Jesus?

Caiaphas, the high priest, declared it would be better for one to die than the whole nation (John 11:49-50). He meant that it would be better for Jesus to die so that they could keep their money and power. Jesus would not only die for the nation of the Jews, but for all people everywhere (John 11:51-52). The Jewish leaders did not approach any situation to determine what was right or wrong morally, but how it would benefit them. How do you face situations in your life? Whether it is politics, finances, social situations, religion or family life — is your first concern: "What would Jesus do?" or "What do I want to do?"

So the Jewish leaders plotted to kill Jesus (John 11:53). Jesus withdrew into the countryside to avoid them at that time (John 11:54). Passover time was near, and the command was given by the chief priests and the Pharisees that Jesus' location was to be reported so that He might be seized (John 11:55-57).

When Jesus raised Lazarus from the dead, He became the threat to the religious system of power and prestige developed by the scribes, priests, Sadducees and Pharisees. They rejected Jesus in spite of all the evidence that He was the Son of God. They plotted to kill Jesus. Jesus was now in the shadow of the cross. The time was near for Jesus to fulfill the purpose for which His Father had sent Him into the world. Obediently, Jesus faced the cross for you and me, and all who would believe.

Jesus would challenge you, "If anyone desires to come after Me, let him deny himself, and take up his cross, and follow Me" (Matthew 16:24). Do you want eternal life? The challenge is clear: Deny yourself, take up your cross and follow Jesus!

CHAPTER 6

THE LAST 7 DAYS
THE LAST WEEK OF JESUS' EARTHLY MINISTRY

DAY 1: THE TRIUMPHAL ENTRY (JOHN 12:1-19)

The sixth section of John's gospel presents the events and teachings of Jesus in His last week of earthly ministry. This section covers Chapters 12-19. The first day is mainly concerned with Jesus' triumphal entry into Jerusalem at the beginning of the Passover celebration. Matthew, Mark, and Luke mention that Jesus went to the temple in Jerusalem. Matthew and Luke declared that Jesus cleansed the temple of all those who were selling animals and exchanging money in the temple area (Luke 19:45-46; Matthew 21:12-13).

When studying the Scripture, it is important to look at the context — that is, the setting of the passage you are studying. The immediate context is Chapter 12, verses 1-11.

It was six days before Passover (John 12:1). Jerusalem was always crowded at Passover. It was the goal of every Jew to observe at least one Passover in Jerusalem. Even today, Jews will say: "This year here, next year Jerusalem." Jesus seemed to always stay at the home of Mary, Martha, and Lazarus when in the area. Bethany was two miles east of Jerusalem. Passover celebrates the Lord's deliverance of Israel from Egyptian slavery.

But the Jews also believed that the Messiah would come at Passover time. Because Jesus had raised Lazarus from the dead, people's expectations were high that Jesus was the Messiah. The hostility of the Jewish authorities was also high. They were seeking to destroy Jesus.

1) The context begins when Jesus came to the home of Mary, Martha, and Lazarus (John 12:1). They prepared supper and Martha was serving as usual. She was a practical woman. Service was her gift. Lazarus was present, the one Jesus had raised from the dead (John 12:2). Mary was also present. She wanted to sit at the feet of Jesus and hear His teaching. Mary took the most precious thing she had and poured the expensive ointment on Jesus' feet and wiped His feet with her hair (John 12:3).

At the time, women would not appear in public with their hair unbound. Their heads were usually covered. This was an act of extravagant love and devotion.

John recalled it was then that Judas, "who would betray Him" (John 12:4), spoke in opposition to the gracious actions of Mary. The "fragrant oil should have been sold for three hundred *denarii* and given to the poor" (John 12:5). One *denarius* was a day's wages for an ordinary worker. The second part of the background deals with Judas.

2) Judas had been given a position of trust by Jesus as their treasurer. He kept the "money box" (John 12:6). If a person has the aptitude for handling money, the temptation comes to regard money as the most important thing in the world. So Judas became a "thief ... and he used to take what was put in it" (John 12:6). Judas was first a thief and then a betrayer of Jesus for thirty pieces of silver, the price of a slave. Judas said the money should be given to the poor. That sounds good. Often people use lofty sounding phrases to paint a good picture of their actions when their true motives are self-centered.

Jesus gave the true meaning of this event in verse 7: "She has kept this for the day of My burial." Jesus was aware of His approaching death, and He knew her anointing was for His burial. "The poor you have with you always ..." (John 12:8). Helping the poor can be done anytime. Those opportunities are always present. But to do this for Jesus was a rare opportunity.

3) The next event that set Jesus' entry into Jerusalem in its proper context was the continuing plotting of the Jewish leaders. They had already put out a "warrant" for His arrest (John 11:57). Now people were coming not only to see Jesus but also to see Lazarus (John 12:9). So the chief priests plotted to also eliminate Lazarus. The priests were Sadducees. The Sadducees did not believe in the resurrection. So the presence of Lazarus was a refutation of their beliefs, so they "plotted to put Lazarus to death also" (John 12:10). Many Jews were believing in Jesus because He had raised Lazarus from the dead (John 12:11).

With popular acclaim for Jesus at its highest point and the anger of the Jewish authorities at fever pitch, the massive celebration of Jesus' entry into Jerusalem is all the more remarkable. Jesus presented Himself as their Messiah and King, and the people responded in praise. The religious leaders felt helpless to stop the celebration.

THE TRIUMPHAL ENTRY

1) The Crowd: Jerusalem was always crowded during the Passover. When Jesus left Bethany to go to Jerusalem, there was a crowd with Him that was bolstered by the news about Jesus raising Lazarus from the dead (John 12:9-11, 17). There was also a crowd that flowed out of Jerusalem to greet Jesus (John 12:18). Many in the crowd probably just wanted to gaze on this miracle-working prophet. It is possible today to draw a crowd by using sensational methods. That doesn't last. This same curious crowd was in a few days shouting for Jesus to be crucified.

2) The Hallel: The crowd greeted Jesus as a conqueror. "Hosanna! Blessed is He who comes in the name of the Lord" (John 12:13). *Hosanna* means "Save now!" The crowd was quoting from Psalm 118:25-26. Psalms 113-118 were called the *Hallel*. *Hallel* means "Praise God." These psalms were a part of the Passover celebration. As the crowd chanted this psalm, they were thinking Jesus was the Messiah, God's Anointed, their Deliverer and King.

3) The Donkey: Jesus rode on a donkey (John 12:14). This action was saying two things to the crowd. One was that Jesus was claiming to be the Messiah, fulfilling the prophecy of Zechariah 9:9: "Behold your King comes to you ... having salvation ... riding upon a donkey." Secondly, Jesus claimed to be a different type of Messiah than what they expected. They wanted a military messiah that would defeat their enemies so they could rule the world. In that time when a king rode a horse, he was going to war. But if the king rode a donkey, he was coming in peace. Jesus came in peace. But in the Book of Revelation, it is written: "Behold, [He comes on] a white horse ..." (Revelation 19:11-16). One day, Jesus will come in judgment.

4) Palm Branches: John mentioned the palm branches in verse 13. To honor an important person like a ruler, the people would wave palm branches and lay them in the road before the procession. Sometimes even clothes were put in the street as the king or high official passed by. The modern equivalent would be rolling out the red carpet for a dignitary. "After these things I looked, and behold, a great multitude which no one could number of all nations, tribes, peoples, and tongues, standing before the throne and before the Lamb, clothed in white robes, with palm branches in their hands, and crying out with a loud voice, saying, "Salvation belongs to our God who sits on the throne, and to the Lamb!" (Revelation 7:9-10). What a joyous celebration that will be!

5) The Jewish Authorities: They were angry, helpless, and frustrated. They cried out, "The whole world is gone after Him" (John 12:19). At the moment their world was proclaiming Jesus to be the Messiah.

Remember, "For God so loved the world" (John 3:16), and now Jesus' enemies thought the world was following Him.

The dominant theme on the first day of Jesus' last week of earthly ministry was praise. The people were chanting: "Hosanna! Blessed is He who comes in the name of the Lord! The King of Israel!" (John 12:13). In Luke 19:39 when the Pharisees heard this praise of Jesus as the Messiah, they said: "Teacher, rebuke Your disciples." But Jesus answered and said: "I tell you that if these should keep silent, the stones would immediately cry out" (Luke 19:40).

I don't want stones giving the praise to the Lord that I should be giving! We all have problems. But if you focus on your problems, your illness, your loneliness, your aches and pains, you will be complaining and not praising. Now the Lord wants us to take all our cares to Him. But Jesus also desires our praise. Begin and end and all through the day, praise the Lord. You might ask, "Now in my distressful situation, why should I praise the Lord?" There are more reasons than I can count. Let's start with praise for our salvation, our eternal life and home in heaven. Praise Jesus for every good thing. Praise Jesus that one day you will have a new body — no more pain, no more sorrow, no more death.

Would you say the dominant theme of your life is praise? If not, make it now. Say with me: "Hallelujah!" "Praise the Lord God!" Praise to the Lord should always be in our hearts and often on our tongues. "My praise shall be continually of You" (Psalm 71:6). And "Let everything that has breath praise the Lord" (Psalm 150:6). Say "Hallelujah!" Say "Hallelujah!" Say "Hallelujah!"

DAY 2: PALM SUNDAY

All four gospel accounts present the triumphal entry of Jesus into Jerusalem on what we call Palm Sunday. Three of the gospels, Matthew,

Mark, and Luke all close out that first day of Jesus' last week of earthly ministry with a visit to the temple. Matthew and Luke wrote that when Jesus came to the temple, He cast out the money changers and animal sellers that were using the court of the Gentiles to conduct business. In both gospels, Jesus quoted from the Scriptures: "My house shall be called a house of prayer" (Isaiah 56:7), and "You have made it a den of thieves" (Jeremiah 7:11). Mark simply recorded that Jesus visited the temple. John does not mention Jesus visiting the temple that day.

In comparing the gospel accounts, it appears that this was the close of the first day. So in John's gospel, the second day of Jesus' last week before the cross would begin in John 12:20.

Following the triumphal entry on day one, there were several important events:

1) The Greeks: Some Greeks were present in Jerusalem, apparently observing Passover. They may have been Jewish converts. However, the Greeks had inquisitive minds and loved to travel. They were also seekers of truth, always wanting to learn something new. When Paul was in Athens preaching Jesus, he was approached by some Epicurean and Stoic philosophers who questioned Paul (Acts 17:18). Luke added this comment: "For all the Athenians and the foreigners who were there spend their time in nothing else but either to tell or to hear some new thing" (Acts 17:21).

2) Jesus foretold His sacrifice (John 12:23-26). God's appointed time for Jesus' sacrificial death on the cross was near (John 12:23). The Jews totally misunderstood. They were looking for a military messiah. One who would defeat all their enemies so they could rule the world. So when Jesus said, "The Son of Man should be glorified" (John 12:23), they thought the Messiah was about to conquer their enemies.

The term "Son of Man" was not new to the Jews. In Daniel 7:1-8, he described great ruling nations as beasts. They were like a lion, a bear, a leopard and like an animal with iron teeth and ten horns. These kingdoms had been cruel and savage, like beasts. But Daniel saw a day coming when a new power would come that was gentle and gracious. He would not be like a beast, but like a man. The Jews believed that this "Son of Man" was their Messiah, the conquering warrior of God. Jesus claimed the title, "Son of Man," because He was the Messiah. But not like they expected. The Jews thought "glorified" referred to the Messiah's conquest of nations. But Jesus' "glory" was to be crucified to conquer sin and death. So Jesus began to speak of sacrifice and death.

The illustration of planting a grain of wheat and producing a harvest was meant to help them understand that in Jesus' death there would be a great harvest of resurrection.

3) Jesus' challenge: Jesus then challenged His hearers with the two possible choices in front of them. The first was if you love this life, you will lose it (John 12:25). But if you hate your life in this world, you will have eternal life (John 12:25). Thinking only of self leads to death. Serving the Lord and others leads to life. Jesus repeated this theme often (Matthew 16:25, 10:39; Mark 8:35; Luke 9:24, 17:33).

True greatness comes by service. In our day, the idea of serving is almost lost. "What's in it for me?" seems to be the most important thing to most people. But true servants of the Lord will be with Jesus one day.

Jesus Predicted the Cross

1) Jesus was "troubled," knowing the cross was coming. John does not record Jesus' agony in Gethsemane, but does reveal Jesus' feelings here. Jesus would not ask the Father to save Him from this, because Jesus knew this was His purpose in coming into the world (John 12:27).

2) The Father glorified: Jesus' desire was that God be glorified. Then the Father spoke from heaven, saying: "I have both glorified it and will glorify it again" (John 12:28). Some bystanders thought it thundered, others thought it was an angel (John 12:29). Jesus wanted them to know the voice came for them to understand (John 12:30). God had also spoken at Jesus' baptism (Mark 1:11) and on the Mount of Transfiguration (Mark 9:7). When Jesus spoke, it was the voice of God. When you read the Bible, God's Word can speak to your heart.

3) Judgment: Judgment had come in Jesus and the ruler of this world would be cast down. Satan was defeated through Jesus' death and resurrection. We can be a part of that victory in Jesus (John 12:31).

4) Jesus and the cross: Jesus declared: "I, if I be lifted up from the earth, will draw all people to Myself" (John 12:33). Jesus was speaking of His death on the cross. The sacrificial death of Jesus opened the door for us to come to the Father.

Jesus Gave an Invitation

1) The Jews had no idea about their Messiah dying. They refused to understand what Jesus was saying (John 12:34).

2) Jesus explained that a little while longer they would have the light, because He was the light. We should stay in the light, live in the light and not in the darkness (John 12:35). Jesus then invited them to believe in the light and become sons of light (John 12:36).

This same invitation is for you. The light of Jesus is present as we have opened His Word and proclaimed His truth to you. Will you believe in Jesus? Do you want to be sons of light rather than remain in the dark? Believe in Jesus now. Trust your life, your heart, your family, your future to the Lord Jesus Christ. We are living in perilous times. The coronavirus pandemic that is worldwide is just a reminder that life is short and we don't know how long we have here. Make a decision to follow Jesus and secure life eternal. Pray now and ask Jesus to forgive you, cleanse you, and change you. Jesus is waiting for you with His arms open wide. Come to Jesus. Come to Jesus now.

DAY 3: 'HARD-HEARTED' (JOHN 12:37-41)

It is impossible to know in John's gospel which verses in Chapter 12 apply to Tuesday or Wednesday. They could apply to either one or both. We can see the ending of day two at the end of verse 36: "These things Jesus spoke, and departed, and was hidden from them." There seems to be another break at the end of verse 41: "These things Isaiah said when he saw His glory and spoke of Him."

So it is possible that verses 37-41 occurred on Tuesday. Although there is no certainty about the specific day to which these verses correspond, what is stated is important for us to study.

THE MAJORITY OF THE JEWS REJECTED JESUS

They did not accept Jesus as the Messiah, the son of God. "Although He had done many signs before them, they did not believe in Him" (John 12:37). John recalled the words of Isaiah, "Lord, who has believed our report? And to whom has the arm of the Lord been revealed?" (John 12:38)

The prophet Isaiah asked if anyone had believed what he had been preaching. He also asked if anyone believed that the power of God (the arm of God) had been revealed (Isaiah 53:1-2). Isaiah was a discouraged prophet. He had proclaimed the Word of the Lord to the people and they had not responded with obedience. They had refused to listen. It was as if they had never heard God's truth. Isaiah was speaking from a broken heart. Instead of repenting and turning to the Lord, the people ignored Isaiah's message and continued in disobedience.

When Jesus approached Jerusalem during his triumphal entry, He "wept over Jerusalem" (Luke 19:41). And in Matthew's gospel, Jesus said: "O Jerusalem, Jerusalem, the one who kills the prophets and stones those who are sent to her! How often I wanted to gather your children together, as a hen gathers her chicks under her wings, but you were not willing!" (Matthew 23:37). Jesus had a deep desire to love, protect, and care for the Jews, but for the most part they rejected Him.

Today, some will not listen, will not respond, will not repent, will not change, and will not choose Jesus. This is tragically sad. It should break our hearts like it did Isaiah's heart and the heart of our Lord.

THE SECOND QUOTE IS FROM ISAIAH 6:10

"He had blinded their eyes and hardened their hearts ... ." This quote had troubled some people. This passage from Isaiah is quoted or understood as a background in Matthew 13:14-15, Mark 4:12, Romans 11:8, and 2 Corinthians 3:14. The witness of the gospels and Paul was that they were faced with the fact of the Jews' rejection of Jesus. As John wrote: "He came into His own, and His own received Him not" (John 1:11). Why did this happen?

1) The freedom to reject: The Lord created us with a free will. The Lord wants us to choose to obey Him. He wants us to decide for ourselves to follow Him. However, the Bible declares: "The Spirit of God will not always strive with men" (Genesis 6:3). There comes a point when the Lord will cease His efforts to draw a person to Himself. You and I do not know when that point will come. Even the two thieves hanging on crosses near Jesus still had an opportunity to believe. One trusted Jesus, the other did not. Why? It is in the heart of an individual person whether they accept or reject Jesus.

2) A good example of Isaiah 6:10 is found in Exodus. When the Lord God sent Moses to Egypt to Pharaoh, saying, "Let my people go," there was a combination of Pharaoh hardening his heart and God confirming Pharaoh's decision. The Scriptures record several times that Pharaoh "hardened his heart" (Exodus 7:13-14; 7:22; 8:15, 19, 32; 9:7, 34, 35). The Scripture also records that God "hardened the heart of Pharaoh"

(Exodus 4:4; 7:3; 9:12; 10:1, 20, 27; 11:10; 14:4, 8, 17).

In Exodus 3:15, the Lord said, "But I am sure that the king of Egypt will not let you go, no, not even by a mighty hand." The Lord knew the heart of Pharaoh. In Exodus 4:21, the Lord confirmed Pharaoh's decision: "I will harden his heart ... ." Another example is in Exodus 7:13-14: "And Pharaoh's heart grew hard, and he did not heed them, as the Lord said. So the Lord said to Moses: 'Pharaoh's heart is hard; he refuses to let the people go.'"

Pharaoh had continually rejected Moses' pleas to release the Hebrew slaves. Pharaoh hardened his heart, and the Lord confirmed his decision. If you continue to reject Jesus, there will be a time — and only the Lord knows when — that He will pass judgment on your decision of rejection (John 5:24).

THE LORD CAN TURN A NEGATIVE INTO A POSITIVE

The truth of Romans 8:28 is vital for us to remember: "And we know that all things work together for good to those who love God, to those who are called according to His purpose." The Lord is always at work moving history to His conclusion. One good outcome of the Jews' rejection of Jesus was that the gospel went to the Gentiles. Paul quoted Isaiah 29:10: "God has given them a spirit of stupor, eyes that they should not see and ears that they should not hear to this very day" (Romans 11:8). Paul went on to write: "I say then, have they stumbled that they should fall? Certainly not! But through their fall, to provoke them to jealousy, salvation has come to the Gentiles" (Romans 11:11). So the good that the Lord brought out of the Jews' rejection of Jesus was that the early church reached out with the gospel to the Gentile world.

THE LORD CAN TURN EVIL INTENTION INTO SOMETHING GOOD

The Lord, in His divine wisdom, can take what people intend for evil and turn it into something good. Joseph was sold into slavery in Egypt by his jealous brothers. In time, Joseph rose to a position second only to Pharaoh in Egypt. When a famine gripped the whole area, Joseph's brothers came to Egypt to buy grain. Finally, Joseph revealed himself to his brothers. They were afraid Joseph would take revenge. But Joseph explained: "But as for you, you meant evil against me, but God meant it for good, in order to bring it about as it is this day, to save many people alive" (Genesis 50:21).

Man's unbelief is not due to God's action. God has not planned for some to be destined for hell. Jesus said: "For God did not send His Son into the world to condemn the world, but that the world through Him might be saved" (John 3:17). When Jesus came, people were faced with a choice — to accept Jesus or reject Him. When they rejected Jesus, they condemned themselves. "He who believes in Him is not condemned; but he who does not believe is condemned already, because he has not believed in the name of the only begotten Son of God" (John 3:18).

How about you? Have you trusted Jesus as Savior and committed your heart and life to Him as Lord? The promise is that those who believe are not condemned, but those who do not believe in Jesus are condemned already.

DAY 4 (JOHN 12:42-50)

We can't know for certain, but it appears that John 12:42-50 refers to day four or Wednesday of Jesus' last week of earthly ministry.

John's comments for this day began with the impossible positions of some of the Jewish rulers: "Many of the rulers believed in Him, but they did not confess Him because of the Pharisees, lest they should be put out of the synagogue" (John 12:42).

Superficial Faith

These rulers had a shallow faith, a superficial faith that was not biblical faith at all. Many people today have their names on the church roll, but do not have a deep, abiding faith in Jesus.

The rulers would have been mainly Sadducees. They were afraid to publicly follow Jesus because they feared that the legalistic Pharisees would excommunicate them. That would have kept them from temple and synagogue worship and basically ostracized them from Jewish society.

So the rulers were trying to be secret disciples. This is impossible. If you are hiding your faith, it is not real faith. A real faith life begins as we allow others to know who we are in Christ. Jesus called His disciples publicly. They had to leave home, family, and work to follow Jesus. John left his father's family fishing business and walked away with Jesus. Faith is something you live, breathe and display. Jesus said: "If anyone desires to come after Me, let him deny himself, take up his cross, and follow Me" (Matthew 16:24).

Are you led by the fads and fashions of this world, or are you following in the footsteps of Jesus? The Christian life should be like a light shining in the darkness. John wrote: "But if we walk in the light as He is in the light, we have fellowship with one another, and the blood of Jesus Christ His Son cleanses us from all sin" (1 John 5:9).

Super Fear

These Jewish rulers were afraid to be open about following Jesus. They must have felt that Jesus was sent from God. They also knew that many of their fellow Jewish leaders wanted to kill Jesus. But they would not risk losing their power or position or wealth by openly declaring their allegiance to Jesus.

How about you? Are you afraid of losing the things of this world if you follow Jesus? Are you concerned about your popularity, your position, your friends, your possessions? Is Jesus more important to you than the stuff of this world?

Ultimate Failure

John understood the heart of these rulers very well. "They loved the praise of men rather than the praise of God" (John 12:43). They were more concerned with what others thought of them than they did what God thought of them. They were educated, wealthy, and prominent men who were supposed to be well versed in the Scriptures. They had no excuse for not following Jesus. They made a decision. They chose to blend into society's morals or lack of them, rather than follow Jesus. They were man pleasers and not God pleasers. Have you decided to follow Jesus or have you drifted into following the ways of the world? Failure — ultimate failure, final failure — is found at the end of the dead-end street called "worldly way"!

Failure Lends to Final Judgment

In John's gospel, these are the final words of Jesus' public ministry. John went on to write about Jesus' instructions to His disciples, words with Pilate, and words from the cross. These verses are Jesus' last words to the public.

1) Jesus declared His oneness with God. He said that anyone who "believes in Me ... believes in Him who sent Me" (John 12:44). He said that anyone who "sees Me, sees Him who sent Me" (John 12:45). When the people encountered Jesus, they were encountering God. John wrote: "In the beginning was the Word and the Word was with God, and the Word was God" (John 1:1). To meet Jesus in faith today is to meet God. The way to the Father is through trusting and obeying Jesus as Lord and Savior.

2) Jesus declared that He is light. Jesus said: "I am [Who I Am] the light of the world" (John 8:12; 9:5). Jesus came into the world as a light shining in the darkness (John 12:46). Jesus, breaking into this world's darkness, gave people the opportunity to believe in Him. This world of darkness would no longer be their home. Jesus said again that His purpose in coming to this world was that people would have the opportunity to believe.

3) Jesus declared His purpose. Jesus did not come to condemn the world. He came to save (John 12:47). Jesus did not come as an angry God to punish people. Jesus did not come in wrath, but He came in love to redeem people. However, the very presence of light reveals the evil deeds of people who love to do their deeds in the darkness. We were watching the news coverage in Nashville on the first day of the rally to protest the death of a man who had died with a policeman's knee on his neck. All was peaceful until darkness came. Then things began to be violent. Mob violence functions mainly in the darkness. "Men love darkness rather than light, because their deeds are evil" (John 3:19).

4) Jesus declared judgment. Jesus said at the "last day" the word that He had spoken will judge the person who has rejected Him and did not receive His words (John 12:48). When a person has heard the truth about Jesus and rejects that truth, he is without excuse. Sin is not just doing what is wrong. It is also knowing what is right to do and failing to do it. The word of truth that you reject will be a witness against you in the day of judgment.

5) Jesus spoke with authority. Jesus made it clear that He was working under the authority of His Father who sent Him (John 12:49). Jesus spoke what His Father commanded Him to speak. Jesus knew the command of His Father is everlasting life (John 12:50). The command, plan, and purpose of the Father is life, not death. "The Lord is ... not willing that any should perish, but that all should come to repentance" (2 Peter 3:9).

John, in summing up Jesus' final public teaching, revealed the themes that Jesus felt were most important for them to remember about Him.

The question is, who is Jesus to you? Was he just a man in ancient history? Just a good man? Perhaps a prophet? A wonderful teacher? An inspiring leader? A martyr in the cause of lifting up the downtrodden?

If you were to sum up what you believe to be true about Jesus, what would you say?

My prayer is that you would say what John said. Jesus is the Son of God, and that Jesus came to save all who would believe in Him. Jesus died on the cross to pay the sin debt. And Jesus is coming again that those who believe in Him may have eternal life. Jesus in the Judge who will return for His faithful followers. And His word is the final judgment on your life. That's what I would say. So, who is Jesus to you?

Day 5, Part 1: Washing The Disciples' Feet (John 13:1-17)

The fifth day or Thursday was a very eventful day. The events and the teaching of Jesus on this day John covered in Chapters 13-17. The Passover began at 6 p.m. on Thursday evening. Jesus and His disciples were preparing to celebrate Passover together (John 13:1). This passage, John 13:1-17, demonstrates the loving character of Jesus in a very striking way. Jesus showed His loving nature in a common, everyday slave task — the washing of feet. Before Jesus washed the disciple's feet, John pointed out that there were four things that Jesus knew.

Four Things Jesus Knew

1) Jesus knew His hour had come. He knew He had come from the Father and that He was going back to the Father (John 13:1). If we were in Jesus' position, we might think, "Good riddance to all the cares and troubles of this world." Jesus had been rejected by His own people. The Jewish authorities were plotting to kill Him. But Jesus "loved His own people in the world" (John 13:11). In spite of the rejection, hostility, and lack of understanding, Jesus still loved. This reveals to us a great truth. The closer we are to the Lord, the more we will love others.

2) Jesus knew He was about to be betrayed. The devil had already put it in the heart of Judas Iscariot to betray Jesus (John 13:2). The devil could not have put this in Judas' heart, if Judas had not wanted it that way. Being betrayed by anyone is very hurtful. But to be betrayed by a close companion of three years — a friend you had worked with, traveled with, and shared meals together with — must be a bitter thing. You and I would resent this wrong if done to us. We might become bitter and plot revenge. But not Jesus!

3) Jesus knew His Father had given Him all things. Jesus knew He had been given all power and authority (John 13:3). Jesus knew the cross was coming, but He knew He would be victorious over death. He knew He would be glorified and ascend the throne as King of kings and Lord of lords. Now if we thought we had all power and authority, it would probably go to our heads. We would assume we were better than others, too important to stop and help others.

4) Jesus knew the heart of the disciples. In Luke's account of the last supper, he wrote: "Now there was also a dispute among them, as to which of them should be considered the greatest" (Luke 22:24). The disciples were concerned about having first place in the kingdom. In their pride they were focusing on their future position instead of Jesus' present mission.

Sometimes we are so concerned about receiving the applause of others or being recognized for our accomplishments that we are not concerned for the needs of others. Will you lower yourself to do a menial task to help someone else?

Washing Feet

There was a simple, lowly task that had been overlooked by the disciples. The roads and streets in Israel were mainly dirt. That means they were very dusty. In wet weather they would have been very muddy. People wore sandals made with soles tied on the feet by leather straps. People kept water pots at the door of their homes. So when people arrived their sandals were removed and their feet washed. The lowest household slave's duty was to wash the feet of those entering the house. In houses without servants, this duty was probably a shared task among family members.

Jesus — knowing the disciples quarrel about who was the greatest, knowing He was going to the Father, knowing He had all power and authority, knowing He was about to be betrayed — took a towel and a basin of water, and began to wash the feet of the disciples. Again, if we were in Jesus' place and knew all these things, we might have rebuked the disciples, given them a stern lecture and walked out! But, no, Jesus washed their feet!

Peter's Refusal

At first, Peter refused to allow Jesus to wash his feet (John 13:6, 8). Jesus told Peter that if he refused this washing, he would have no part with Jesus. Then Peter also wanted his hands and head to be washed (John 13:9)! Jesus explained that only his feet needed to be washed (John 13:10). It was the custom that before people went to feast that they bathed themselves. When they arrived at the host's home, all that was needed was to have their feet washed. The washing of the feet was the ceremony that allowed entry into the house. If Peter had been too proud for Jesus to do that for him, his pride would have kept him out of the kingdom. Some people are too proud to walk the aisle, too proud to be baptized, too proud to think that they need anyone to die for them, too proud to humble themselves at the feet of Jesus and receive eternal life. Will your pride stand between you and Jesus?

TEACHING ABOUT GREATNESS

The comment from Luke's gospel about who will be the greatest seems to be the background for verses 13-17. Jesus knew about their quarrel. That controversy is why none of the disciples would wash the other disciple's feet. None of them had been willing to humble themselves and perform this lowly task.

That is why when Jesus had finished this illustration of love and humility, He asked: "Do you know what I have done to you?" (John 13:12). Jesus did what none of the disciples were willing to do. Jesus said: "You call me Master and Lord, and you are right" (John 13:13). Jesus was their Lord and Master, yet He washed their feet! A student does not deserve more honor than the teacher. A servant does not deserve more honor then the master (John 13:16). Yet Jesus, the Master, served His servants!

We need to grow in our understanding as well. Sometimes in churches people cause trouble when they do not receive the recognition or the place they think they deserve. Some pastors are offended because they feel they did not receive the honor due them.

There is only one kind of greatness, according to Jesus. True greatness is found in service. The world is full of people puffed up with their own self-importance. Real greatness is not found in standing in prominent places, but in kneeling at the feet of Jesus. Real greatness is not found in standing up for your position, but in kneeling down to help a brother in distress. Real greatness is not in being recognized as a prominent person, but rather serving others unnoticed.

When we begin thinking about our place, our rights, our position, we need to remember Jesus, the Son of God, taking a towel, a basin of water, and washing the feet of His disciples. Real greatness is found in humble service.

Paul challenged us: "Let this mind be in you which was also in Christ Jesus, who, being in the form of God did not consider it robbery to be equal with God …. . And being found in appearance as a man, He humbled Himself and became obedient to the point of death, even the death of the cross" (Philippians 2:5-6, 8).

Have you humbled yourself at the feet of Jesus?

Day 5, Part 2: 'The Betrayal Predicted' (John 13:18-30)

Judas' betrayal of Jesus has always been a mystery to me. How could anyone do that to a friend? How could anyone do that to Jesus, who was the loving, kind and generous Savior? Growing up, I was at a loss as to how Judas could do such a terrible deed. I must admit as I have grown older, I am still perplexed that a person could do that to Jesus.

Jesus Revealed His Betrayal

1) Cruel disloyalty: Jesus warned the disciples about His coming betrayal so that they would understand and not be overwhelmed when it happened (John 13:18). To put His betrayal in perspective, Jesus quoted Psalm 41:9. The complete verse is: "Even my own familiar friend in whom I trusted, who ate my bread, has lifted up his heel against me." Three things in this verse help explain how cruel this betrayal was.

   a) "My bread" signified the value placed upon the bond that was expressed in a shared meal. In the Middle East, when you ate a meal with a person, it was a sign of friendship and loyalty. According to Old Testament law, even a stranger passing through your land was under your protection. An example is

David's kindness to Mephibosheth: "So David said to him, "Do not fear, for I will surely show you kindness for Jonathan your father's sake, and will restore to you all the land of Saul your grandfather, and you shall eat bread at my table continually" (2 Samuel 9:7).

b) "My own familiar friend" signified the closeness of the relationship. The person was not an enemy, an acquaintance, or a stranger, but a friend. To have a close friend to betray you is a bitter thing.

c) "Lift up his heel" signified brutal violence. This phrase is literally "make great the heel." It is similar to our phrase, "kicking a person when he is down." Jesus' appeal was to let Judas know how hurt He would be. This is not anger, but Jesus was simply explaining the sorrow He felt.

2) Within the plan of God: Jesus' betrayal was part of the plan of God. Jesus said, "That the Scripture may be fulfilled ..." (John 13:18). Redemption was only going to happen when the perfect sacrifice for sin was offered. The perfect sacrifice was Jesus, the perfect Son of God. No one was going to take His life from Him, Jesus was going to give His life a ransom for many (Mark 10:45). The disciples did not understand all this then, but later they would remember and understand. By Jesus having this foreknowledge of future events, the disciples would believe that Jesus is "I Am Who I Am" (John 13:19).

The Glory of Faithfulness

The time would come when these disciples would take the gospel out to the world. They would be representing the Lord God wherever they went. Paul wrote: "We are ambassadors for Christ as though God were pleading through us, we implore you on Christ's behalf, be reconciled to God" (2 Corinthians 5:20). An ambassador does not represent

himself, but his country's government. It is an honor to represent Christ
in a lost world. We speak for Jesus as we share the Word of God with
others (John 13:20).

WHO WAS THE BETRAYER?

Jesus revealed that the betrayer was one of the disciples (John
13:21). The disciples all looked at each other, but could not discern who
it was (John13:22). Who was it? We know it was Judas. But Judas was
a hypocrite. The word "hypocrite" comes from the masks or false faces
the Greek actors wore so the audience in the large amphitheaters would
know if their character was happy or sad. The word came to mean
"actor." So a hypocrite is someone who pretended to be someone other
than who he really is. Judas had all the disciples fooled. It seems Judas
was never suspected, because he could act like a saint, but his allegiance
was to the devil. You and I can deceive other people, but we can never
deceive Jesus.

JESUS REACHED OUT IN LOVE TO JUDAS

Jesus knew the heart of Judas. He must have seen the potential in
Judas to be a worthy disciple, but Judas' heart was more concerned with
material gain than it was in following Jesus. Jesus appealed to Judas at
least three ways.

*1) Jesus had given Judas a very responsible role as treasurer of the
group.* The other disciples never suspected Judas of any wrong doing
until after Judas' betrayal of Jesus (John 12:6)

2) Jesus gave Judas the place of honor at the Passover meal. It is
important to understand the meal arrangements in Jesus' day. They did
not sit in chairs at a high table to eat. They reclined on cushions on the
floor leaning on their left elbow at a low table. Their body would be
extended out behind them. Lying in such a way a person's head was at

the chest of the person on their left. The disciple "whom Jesus loved" (John 13:23) has always been believed to be John himself. Jesus was the host, so John was reclining to Jesus' right (John 13:25). Then Peter asked John, who was next to Jesus, to ask who the betrayer was (John 13:24). John asked Jesus: "Lord, who is it?" (John 13:25). Jesus answered: "It is he to whom I shall give a piece of bread when I have dipped it" (John 13:26).

It is clear that for Judas to receive this special piece of bread, he would have had to be close. Judas must have been reclining on Jesus' left. Jesus' head would have been near Judas' chest. The place on the left of the host was the place of highest honor. This position was always reserved for the most honored guest. This was a gracious act by Jesus to appeal to Judas.

3) Another special favor was for the host to offer to someone the first food from the dish. It is still a custom for most of us to serve our guests first. It showed a special appeal to offer this first serving to Judas. The other disciples thought nothing of this. Up to this point, apparently Judas was well thought of by the disciples.

Again and again, Jesus appealed to Judas. But Judas' heart was hardened. He must have been so focused on monetary gain that all of Jesus' appeals meant nothing to him (John 13:27). Jesus told Judas: "What you do, do quickly" (John 13:27). At that moment, Jesus knew it was useless to keep trying. Why prolong the agony? So Jesus basically said: "If this is what you are determined to do, do it quickly."

The disciples suspected nothing (John 13:28). The disciples reasoned that something else was needed for the feast or that an offering needed to be made for the poor (John 13:29).

IT WAS NIGHT

When Judas took the food from Jesus, the devil entered Judas. The devil can twist something good into something evil. Corn is a good vegetable to eat, but it was not meant to be drunk like moonshine! Satan can take love and turn it into lust. Satan can take service and turn it into pride.

So Judas left: "And it was night" (John 13:30). John had a way of using words to not only state the facts, but also to portray the spiritual impact of the moment. It was late, so it was night. Judas, in turning his back on Jesus, walked away from the light into the darkness. It is always night when you turn your back on Jesus. It is always night when you listen to Satan instead of Jesus. It is always night when you go your way instead of Jesus' way. It is always night when you listen to the world and turn a deaf ear to the Word of God. It is always night when you accept the morals of Hollywood and reject the holiness of God. It is always night when you adopt a worldly lifestyle and abandon godly living.

My heart's desire is that I will always walk in the light with Jesus and not in the darkness with the Judas crowd. How about you? Are you walking with Jesus in the light, or are you walking with the worldly crowd in spiritual darkness? Maybe you are being tempted to turn to the dark side? You need to pray: "Jesus, I believe that you are the Son of God and that You died on the cross to pay for my sins and rose again that I might have eternal life. I repent of my sins, and I want to walk in the light of Your love."

DAY 5, PART 3: 'THE SON OF MAN IS GLORIFIED' (JOHN 13:31-38)

In day five of Jesus' last week before the cross, John included many events and teachings of Jesus. Jesus was preparing the disciples for the time when He would no longer be with them. The verses we are studying today center around the coming cross of Jesus. We would not normally associate the word "glory" with death. We would not associate the word "glory" with the electric chair. So why should there be glory in the cross? Both the cross and the electric chair are instruments for the execution of criminals.

THE GLORY OF THE CROSS

John wrote: "So, when he (Judas) had gone out ..." (John 13:31). When Judas left, the tension was gone, the doubts were gone, the betrayer was gone! Have you ever felt the presence of evil? Some years ago, Joy and I were flying to Salt Lake City to attend the annual meeting of the Southern Baptist Convention. We had to change planes in the airport in Las Vegas. The airport lobby was filled with slot machines. The aura of evil was oppressive. Have you heard the expression, "The fog was so thick you could cut it with a knife"? The feeling of evil was so thick you could have cut it with a knife.

"Now the son of Man is glorified ..." (John 13:31). The time had come. "Now" the Son of Man was to be glorified on the cross. The cross was a certainty. Jesus was ready to go willingly to the cross for you and me and for all who would believe in Jesus Christ as the Lord and Savior. Jesus' sacrificial death on the cross was His glory. Our greatest glory also comes from sacrifice.

I have a friend, Jerry Currey, whom I have known for over thirty-five years. He was wounded severely in Vietnam. I called him a hero one day, and he said: "The real heroes are the ones who never came back." Jerry has shared his testimony many times in many churches. During the war, Jerry's camp came under enemy fire. A soldier was hit, and he was out in the open. Jerry got to him and placed him in a medical helicopter. On the way back to his bunker, a mortar shell went off at Jerry's feet. He lost one leg, and the other was severely damaged. Shrapnel went throughout his body, and he was blinded by the blast. While lying there, Jerry prayed, "Lord, if you will let me live, I will live for you." After many months in the hospital, Jerry came home. He has served as a deacon in his church, and shared the gospel in visiting with families in their homes. Jerry's sacrifice, like so many others, should not be forgotten.

The Glory of Obedience

Jesus glorified His Father through His obedience (John 13:32). Jesus had stated that His purpose in coming to this world was the cross (John 12:27). Also, in Jesus, God glorified Himself (John 13:32). In Jesus, God revealed His true nature. Our God revealed Himself to be loving, caring, and compassionate. He showed Himself in Jesus to be Lord over nature, illness, disease, and death. Our loving Heavenly Father is involved in our lives for our good (Romans 8:28).

Because Jesus obediently went to the cross, He wears the crown. What seemed like a defeat at the cross was revealed as a victory at the resurrection. The crown of thorns is now a crown of glory. Jesus is King of kings and Lord of lords. Obedience to Jesus is not an option, but is essential if we are to be true followers of Christ.

The Commandment to Love

The last commandment Jesus gave the disciples before the cross was to love one another (John 13:34). Jesus told them again that He would soon leave them. Sadly, at that time they could not go with Him (John 13:33). Jesus then gave them a powerful command "to love one another." This commandment from Jesus had three important components:

1) It was a commandment to love with God's kind of love. The word for "love" is the word always associated with God's kind of love. This love meant to always want what is best for the other person. It is not a selfish or self-centered love, but a love that cares for others.

2) A second important component of the command to love one another is the statement, "As I have loved you." They were commanded to imitate the love that Jesus had for them. Jesus' caring, unselfish, under-standing, forgiving and sacrificial love was best seen on the cross. That's the kind of love we are to have for one another.

3) *The command to love one another will be a powerful witness to all people (John 13:35).* People will recognize that you are a true disciple of the Lord Jesus Christ when you demonstrate your love for one another. Love is the one true indicator that you are a believer in Jesus. For without love, you are just "sounding brass or clanging cymbal," Paul wrote in 1 Corinthians 13:1.

Is your life characterized by forgiveness, understanding, sacrifice and unselfishness? If not, it is not the love of Jesus.

PETER'S DECLARATION OF LOYALTY

1) *Peter avoided the mention of the new commandment "to love one another as I have loved you" and returned to the idea of Jesus going away.* Apparently Peter did not understand. So Peter asked: "Lord, where are you going?" (John 13:36). Jesus answered that Peter could not follow Him now, but that in the future Peter could follow. Dying on the cross for our sins was something only Jesus could do. Jesus had to conquer sin, hell, and death first in order for Peter and others to follow.

Peter still did not understand and asked again: "Why not now? I will die for you" (John 13:37). I believe Peter was sincere and had an earnest desire to stay with Jesus. Still not understanding that the cross was something only Jesus could do, Peter thought he was courageous enough to die for Jesus. Jesus responded that Peter would deny Him three times before the rooster crowed (John 13:38).

2) *There were two tragic actions by two of Jesus' disciples as Jesus neared the cross.* One was Judas' betrayal, and the other was Peter's denial. These actions had different outcomes. Judas hung himself, and Peter went on to be a great leader in the early church. What was the difference?

Judas deliberately plotted to betray Jesus for personal monetary gain. He was later overcome with remorse and hung himself. Peter talked boldly. Peter had good intentions, but he was weak. Peter did not plan to deny Jesus, but in a moment of fear and weakness he did. Peter wept bitterly over his betrayal. But Peter stayed. Jesus, after the resurrection, had the opportunity to lovingly restore Peter.

Jesus knew His disciples. Jesus knew them, yet He loved them anyway. Jesus knows all about you, yet He loves you anyway. You might have a high opinion of someone, but when you learn their weaknesses and faults, you might change your opinion. Real love, like Jesus' love, accepts a person as they are. That doesn't mean that you don't want them to grow in Christlikeness, to mature in the faith and become the best person they can possibly be.

Part of the marriage vows that those of you who are married probably repeated are: "For better or worse, richer or poorer, in sickness and in health … ." Do you remember? "Real Jesus love" does not forget the marriage vows or any other pledge you have made. If you have "real Jesus love," your pledge to take up your cross and follow Jesus is a pledge you intend to keep.

DAY 5, PART 4: 'THE PROMISE OF HEAVEN' (JOHN 14:1-6)

In a short time, the disciples' world was going to collapse. Fear, sorrow and chaos would soon take control of their lives. Have you ever felt like that? There is an old saying that expresses this feeling well. It is like "being caught between a rock and a hard place." Years ago, after having a very stressful day, I remarked to my wife, Joy, "I feel like I have been run over by a Mack truck." I think most of us have been in that circumstance. Right now with COVID-19, high unemployment, and social unrest, America is between a rock and a hard place.

What should our nation do in this time of crisis? What should you do when your personal world is falling apart? The only way out is to trust in the Lord. In Psalm 27:13, we read, "I had fainted, unless I had believed to see the goodness of the Lord in the land of the living." Real hope springs from faith in the mercy and grace of the Lord and His promise of our future home.

JESUS' CURE FOR TROUBLED HEARTS

1) An encouraging word: Jesus understood the anxious hearts of His disciples. Jesus sought to encourage them ahead of time for the difficult days of anguish and separation. So very kindly, Jesus said: "Let not your heart be troubled ..." (John 14:1). In difficult times, Jesus had approached the disciples saying, "Fear not" (Matthew 10:31; Luke 5:10, 8:50, 12:7, 12:32).

When you are troubled, anxious, or distressed, listen as Jesus speaks to your heart, saying, "Fear not!" The beginning of your deliverance from stressful circumstances is to listen to Jesus' words of comfort. We can stand with others in their times of trouble with a word of comfort and hope from the Lord.

2) A challenge of faith: Jesus followed His word of encouragement with a challenge to believe in God and also to believe in Him: "Believe in God, believe also in Me" (John 14:1). As believers, we are to live by faith. We see how essential that is when life tumbles in, when the darkness comes, when friends turn away, or our health fails. Our faith in Jesus is the only hope that sustains us. We must believe in Jesus when there seems to be no way. Jesus is the waymaker. He is the light in an otherwise dark world.

Many people claim that they believe in God. Too often, it is a god of their own making. Jesus came to reveal the Father. Jesus said: "I and My Father are one." In Jesus, we realize God's amazing grace and everlasting love.

A Promise of a Heavenly Home

"In My Father's house are many mansions …" (John 14:2). The word "mansions" is literally "dwellings." In heaven, there is room for all who believe. The inn in Bethlehem was too crowded when Jesus was about to be born. But Jesus has room for you. You may have been on a road trip and seen "No Vacancy" signs on some motels. God's love has no boundaries. There is room in the Father's house for all who come by faith in the Lord Jesus Christ. There is still room for you, if you will come to Jesus in repentance and faith.

A Promise We Can Depend On

We can depend upon this promise of a heavenly home because Jesus, the great "I Am Who I Am," said so. Jesus said: "If it were not so, I would have told you" (John 14:2). Jesus always tells it like it is. Jesus did not try to lure people into following Him by making false promises for an easy life or great riches. Jesus said: "Foxes have holes and birds of the air have nests, but the Son of Man has nowhere to lay His head" (Luke 9:58), and "In the world you will have tribulation; but be of good cheer, I have overcome the world" (John 16:33).

Jesus told the truth. Jesus said: "I am the way, the truth, and the life …" (John 14:6). I discussed this "I Am Who I Am" saying of Jesus at length earlier in our study of the seven "I Am Who I Am" sayings of Jesus. Jesus not only tells the truth, He is the truth! Jesus not only can show us the way to the Father, He is the way! Jesus not only can teach us the real meaning of life, He is life and can give you eternal life!

A Promise to Prepare a Place

Jesus said: "I go to prepare a place for you" (John 14:2). Like a good shepherd, Jesus has gone before us to prepare a place for us. In Hebrews 6:20, it says of Jesus: "The forerunner has entered for us, even Jesus, having become High Priest forever according to the order of Melchizedek." The word "forerunner" was used for the scout troops of the Roman army. They went ahead of the main army to mark a safe trail in ancient harbors, with difficult channels, a pilot boat was used to safely guide large ships into the harbor. The pilot boat was called the "forerunner." This was true in early America, where men like Daniel Boone blazed a trail for others to follow.

Jesus is the forerunner who has made a way from this earthly life to eternal life in heaven.

A Promise to Come for Us

Jesus said: "And if I go and prepare a place for you, I will come again and receive you to Myself" (John 14:3). The second coming of Jesus seems to be largely ignored in churches today. Jesus promised to come again, so it will happen. Since we don't know when Jesus is coming, many people think nothing about it. Some take the idea to the extreme with charts and calculations of the exact time of Jesus' return. Jesus said: "But of that day and hour no one knows, not even the angels of heaven, but My Father only" (Matthew 24:36). Jesus is coming! We must be ready! Jesus said: "Watch therefore, for you do not know what hour your Lord is coming" (Matthew 24:42).

A Promise that We Will Be with Jesus

Jesus said that "where I am, there you may be also" (John 14:3). Heaven is to be with Jesus. We don't know all the details about heaven. We don't need to know everything. The most important point is that we will be with Jesus. As believers, we have had what we call "mountaintop experiences" with the Lord. But as frail human beings, we are not always aware of Jesus' presence. Just imagine that in heaven you will be in His presence forever. Nothing will ever come between you and the Lord.

While I was writing this, a young lady to whom my wife, Joy, has been a spiritual mentor for years sent us a text. Simone Wofford, who has a beautiful voice, wanted to come and sing for Joy. At the time, Joy was recovering from five strokes that happened eight months earlier. Because of the coronavirus, Simone stood in our driveway, and, with her computer and small speaker for an orchestra, she sang us four songs. She sang one of Joy's favorites. One line in the song is: "Let not your heart be troubled, His tender word I hear. And resting on His goodness, I lose my doubts and fears; … His eye is on the sparrow, and I know He watches me."

DAY 5, PART 5: 'JESUS AND THE FATHER' (JOHN 14:7-11, 19-24, 28-31; 16:16-22)

John, more than the other gospels, emphasized the unique oneness of Jesus and the Father. John's gospel began: "In the beginning was the Word, and the Word was with God and the Word was God" (John 1:1). This relationship between God the Father and God the Son is especially emphasized in Chapters 14-17. The name "Father" appears forty-eight times in these chapters alone. In Jesus' last teaching opportunities before the cross, He wanted His disciples to really grasp who He was. The first passage we will focus on is John 14:7-11.

GOD IN THE FLESH

The Jews believed that no one had ever seen God. God spoke to Moses, but did not allow Moses to see His face: "You shall see my back;

but My face shall not be seen" (Exodus 33:23).

Jesus stated plainly that in Him they had seen the Father (John 14:7). Philip then asked: "Lord, show us the Father ..." (John 14:8). Jesus responded that Philip should have known who He was (John 14:9). Then again, Jesus stated clearly: "He who has seen Me has seen the Father" (John 14:9). To see Jesus was to see God. To see Jesus was to see what God is like. As you read about Jesus in the gospels, you are reading about the words and actions of God.

"The Word became flesh and dwelt among us" (John 1:14). God took upon Himself human form and faced the difficulties of life just like we have to do. When God came into this world as a human baby, He sanctified human birth and human life. Abortion is a destructive evil. Some say abortion is a choice, but even in our society when one person chooses to murder another, it is illegal and punishable by law. The exception to this rule of law is the murdering of unborn children!

As Jesus taught, as Jesus healed, God was visible. When Jesus died on the cross, the loving heart of God was revealed. Jesus is the revelation of God.

The danger for Christians is that we may think of Jesus as a second God. Many times Jesus stated that what He said and what He did all came from the Father. His power and authority were God's (John 14:10). Through Jesus, God came to us. Jesus brought God's heart, mind, grace, mercy and message to us.

Again, Jesus clearly stated: "It is the Father who dwells in me. ... I am in the Father and the Father is in Me" (John 14:10). Jesus called upon them to believe what He said (John 14:10). Jesus also called upon them to believe because of His works (John 14:11). Jesus healed sick bodies, sick minds, and even raised the dead. Only God could do those things.

The Father Will Dwell in Believers

In John 14:1-24, Jesus included believers in this indwelling relationship with the Father. It began with Jesus continuing to help the disciples understand that He would soon leave them (John 14:19). Although the disciples would no longer see Him, Jesus declared: "Because I live, you will live also" (John 14:19). Jesus then gave a powerful promise in verse 20: "I am in My Father, and you in Me, and I in you." Believers will enter into a new relationship with God, in which believers are in Christ and Christ is in the believer! This new relationship is based on two things:

1) Love: "God is love." The Father loves Jesus, and when we love Jesus we enter into a new relationship of love with the Father (John 14:21). Believers became included in this bond of love.

2) Obedience: "He who has My commandments and keeps them, it is He who loves Me" (John 14:21). Obedience to Jesus opens your heart to be indwelled by the Father and the Son (John 14:23). The word translated "home" means "to take up residence." God will dwell in the heart of the faithful. Jesus said: "And the word that you hear is not mine, but the Father's who sent Me" (John 14:24). Love of the Father results in obedience.

Jesus Invites Us into His Circle of Love

In John 14:28-31, Jesus again reminded His disciples that He was going away, but that He was coming back to them (John 14:28). If the disciples really understood and loved Jesus, they would rejoice that He was going to the Father. When our Christian loved ones die, we miss them. The separation of death brings sorrow, but at the same time we can rejoice because they have gone to be with the Lord.

Jesus explained that He was telling all of this to them ahead of time so they would believe (John 14:29). Jesus told them that the "prince of this world," Satan, was coming (John 14:30). Satan-inspired hatred of Jesus would soon move people to shout, "Crucify Him!" But Satan has no control over Jesus (John 14:30). Although Satan may have thought that he had won when Jesus was on the cross, the end result was Jesus' victory over Satan, sin, hell, and death. The cross demonstrated Jesus' love and obedience to the Father (John 14:31). When we are obedient to the Word of God, we declare to the world that we love Jesus. The result of our love of Jesus will always be obedience. If there is no obedience, there is no love.

Back in the early 1990s, there began a Christian men's movement called "Promise Keepers." Men from our church attended many of these events. In one of the early rallies, men on one side of the packed arena started chanting loudly: "We love Jesus, yes we do; we love Jesus, how about you?" They pointed to another section of men, and those men would respond in like manner. It is important to tell others we love Jesus, but it means nothing if we don't obey Him. Jesus wants us to be in the circle of His love.

Sorrow Turned into Joy

In John 16:16-22, Jesus again told the disciples that He was going away: "In a little while you will not see me anymore, and again in a little while you will see Me because I go to the Father" (John 16:16). The disciples did not understand the phrase "a little while" or Jesus saying, "I am going to My Father (John 16:17). Jesus knew what was troubling His disciples (John 16:19). Jesus knew the cross was coming soon. Jesus' death would separate Him from the disciples for a "little while." During that time, they would weep and lament, but the world (all those without the Lord) would be rejoicing. But in a "little while," the disciples' grief would be turned to joy (John 16:20).

Jesus then gave the example of a woman in labor at childbirth. Once the child is born, the joy of the newborn baby helps her forget her pain

(John 16:21). The disciples would have grief, but when they would see Jesus again, they would rejoice, and "no one will take your joy from you" (John 16:22).

The world seeks happiness. The English word "happiness" comes from the word *hap*, meaning "chance." "Joy" is a gift from the Lord. This deep inner sense of joy can never be taken away from you (John 16:22, 15:11). The ultimate joy will be to see Jesus in heaven one day. All past sorrow and pain will be forgotten. Your faith relationship with Jesus results in joy.

Do you have the joy of the Lord in your heart? Nothing this world has to offer can produce joy. Neither money, fame, power, position, nor prestige can fill the void in your heart. That void can only be filled by the presence of Jesus and His gift of joy.

Do you have the joy of Jesus down in your heart, down in your heart to stay?

DAY 5, PART 6: 'PRAYER' (JOHN 14:12-14; 16:23-24; 16:25-28)

Jesus had a strong desire that His disciples would learn to pray. Jesus had said that prayers did not have to be long (Matthew 23:14). Prayers should not be made on street corners to be seen by others; prayers should not be pretentious or prideful (Matthew 6:5). For example, Jesus told a story of a Pharisee who went to the temple to pray. Jesus said, "The Pharisee ... prayed thus with himself, 'God, I thank You that I am not like other men — extortioners, unjust, adulterers or even as this tax collector. I fast twice a week; I give tithes of all that I possess" (Luke 18:10-12).

Jesus also gave His disciples a sample prayer they could imitate. This prayer that we call "the Lord's Prayer" was brief, but it contains the major points of prayer (Matthew 6:9-13). The prayer is addressed to "our Father" and praises His name. The requests begin with God's will being done on earth as it is in heaven, followed by requests for food and forgiveness, and that we would avoid temptation and be delivered from evil. The prayer ends with praise. With this background in mind, let's turn to the passages in John's gospel where Jesus taught His disciples about prayer.

Ask in My Name

The next passage we will study is John 14:12-14. Jesus said: "If you ask Me anything in My name, I will do it" (John 14:12). We must be careful to understand what Jesus meant. He did not say anything we ask will be granted, but what we ask "in His name." Names were especially important in Bible times. The name represented the character and reputation of the person. So the question we must ask ourselves is: Is my prayer in line with the name, the character, and the purpose of Jesus? Prayers for personal revenge, personal ambition, personal greed, or any unchristlike thing will not be answered. Selfish prayers will not be answered. The real Lord's prayer was prayed in the Garden of Gethsemane: "Not My will, but Yours, be done" (Luke 22:42).

The Father Will Answer

The second passage on prayer is found in John 16:23-24. Jesus said: "The Father will give you in My name whatever you will ask Him." In the context of these two verses, Jesus was explaining again that He was going to the Father. We have discussed verses 16-22 earlier. Jesus sought to encourage His followers with the astonishing truth that even though He would be visibly absent, they could talk to the Father, in His name.

The disciples would have a new relationship with the Father. They knew about Him, because they knew Jesus. They could understand the heart, mind, and character of the Father because they knew Jesus. So when Jesus was gone, they could communicate with the Father in Jesus' name. As His children, we know our Heavenly Father welcomes us into His presence with open arms. Again, the idea of receiving whatever we ask Him is conditioned by the fact that what we ask must be in keeping with the name and character of Jesus.

YOUR JOY WILL BE COMPLETE

The joy that we receive from the Lord is "complete," or "perfect" (John 16:24). This means that the Lord's joy lacks nothing. As we have discussed before, this joy can never be taken away (John 16:22). That joy is present in our lives because Jesus is present. Jesus promised to "never leave you nor forsake you" (Hebrews 13:5). Nothing can separate us from the love of the Lord Jesus Christ.

DIRECT ACCESS TO THE FATHER

In John 16:25-28, Jesus continued explaining the new relationship the disciples would have with the Father. Jesus said: "The hour is coming when ... I will tell you plainly about the Father" (John 16:25).

A new concept that Jesus told His disciples was that they would have direct access to the Father. If you wanted to speak to a king or a queen, you would need an official invitation or someone to intercede for you to gain an audience with royalty. Jesus declared that He did not have to "pray to the Father for you" (John 16:26), because "the Father Himself loves you" (John 16:27). Since we have a loving Heavenly Father, we can take our requests directly to Him in Jesus' name.

Some think of God as an angry, judgmental God, but Jesus is loving and caring. Before Jesus went to the cross, He explained to His disciples that the Father loved them. Remember, Jesus came into the world, not because God hated the world, but because "God so loved the world"

(John 3:16). We would never have understood the love of God without Jesus coming into our world, living and teaching, and dying on the cross. Through Jesus, the heart of God was revealed.

Our part in coming into this new relationship with the Father is that we love Jesus and believe He came from the Father (John 16:27). Jesus told them that He came from the Father and He was going back to the Father (John 16:28). This is a clear claim that Jesus is the Son of God and that He did not die a criminal's death on the cross, but He paid the penalty for our sin and returned to His Father.

Jesus' earthly work was finished on the cross. He was going home, but Jesus had opened a way to the Father. We have access to the Father through Jesus. We can take our praises and petitions directly to the Father.

Two 'I Am Who I Am' Sayings of Jesus

1) When we studied the seven "I Am Who I Am" sayings of Jesus, we remember Jesus said: "I am [Who I Am] the way, the truth, and the life" (John 14:6). Not only does Jesus know the way to the Father, He is the Way. Not only does Jesus know the truth, He is the Truth. Not only is Jesus the source of life, He is the giver of eternal Life. Through faith, we can enter into a new relationship with the Father because of Jesus.

2) Jesus also said: "I am [Who I Am] the true vine, and My Father is the vinedresser" (John 15:1). We must be attached to the vine in order to have life and bear fruit. Branches that do not bear fruit are cut off, but those that bear fruit are cleansed so they can bear more fruit (John 15:2). Jesus was emphasizing our need to abide in Him (John 15:4). Because we abide in Jesus, we may "ask what you desire, and it shall be done for you" (John 15:7).

These two sayings of Jesus help us understand our position with the Lord and our privilege of praying in Jesus' name.

Jesus' Great Prayer

In Chapter 17, Jesus prayed a wonderful prayer that we will study later. But quickly, in that prayer, Jesus prayed for Himself as He faced the cross. He prayed for the disciples and for God's power to sustain them. He prayed for you! Jesus prayed for all those who would believe in the future.

True Prayer

True prayer contains these elements: Adoration or praise, confession, thanksgiving, and supplication. Easy to remember. Take the first letter of each one, and it spells ACTS! Prayer is effective when we pray in the name of Jesus — that is, when we pray according to the will, purpose, and plan of the Lord. Our prayers must line up with the will and character of our Lord Jesus Christ.

When was the last time you really prayed? I know there are times of urgent, emergency requests when we cry out to the Lord. Do you take time to praise Him, confess your sins, thank Him for all His many blessings and then bring your requests to Him?

One of the most wonderful privileges of being a child of the King is that we can approach His throne of grace and talk to our Savior and Lord in prayer.

Day 5, Part 7: 'The Holy Spirit' (John 14:15-18, 25-27; 16:5-15)

In the last several sections, we have been discussing the teachings of Jesus on the fifth day, Thursday, of His last week of earthly ministry. Jesus had told the disciples that He was going to leave them and return to His Father. The disciples would then have a new relationship with the Father. Since Jesus was going away, He taught them about prayer.

Although Jesus would be apart from them, they could pray to the Father. They would have direct access to the Father in prayer in the name of Jesus. Because Jesus was physically leaving them, He promised not to leave them alone. He promised that the Holy Spirit would come and dwell in them.

THE PROMISE OF THE SPIRIT

In John 14:16, Jesus promised them the presence of the Holy Spirit. There were two prior conditions that must be met. The first was to love Jesus, and the second was to keep the commandments (John 14:15). When these two conditions were given, Jesus said He would "pray the Father, and He will give you another Helper ..." (John 14:16). There are three words that we need to examine:

1) The word "another" means "another of the same kind." In the Bible the Holy Spirit is also called the "Spirit of God" and the "Spirit of Christ." So the Holy Spirit is just like Jesus, just like God. "God is Spirit, and those who worship Him must worship in spirit and truth" (John 4:24). In a concept that is difficult to comprehend, we have one Lord who has revealed Himself to us in different ways.

2) The word translated "Helper" literally meant "one called along side of." If you are sick, you would call a physician to your side to help you. If you were in legal trouble, you would call a lawyer to come to your side to help you. So the Holy Spirit is able to come alongside of us to help us in any situation. The Holy Spirit helps us cope with life.

3) The word translated "abide" means "to take up residence" (John 14:16). The Holy Spirit will come into the heart of the believer and live in them forever (John 14:16). Jesus also said: "My Father will love him, and We will come to him and make our home with him" (John 14:23). We are called to abide in Jesus and Jesus will abide in us (John 15:4). When we abide in Jesus, the door of prayer is open (John 15:7).

THE HOLY SPIRIT IS THE SPIRIT OF TRUTH

In John 14:17, the Helper is called the Spirit of truth and "He dwells with you and will be in you." There are four works of the Holy Spirit that are mentioned:

1) Testify of Jesus: John 15:26 states, "But when the Helper comes, whom I will send to you from the Father, the Spirit of Truth who proceeds from the Father, He will testify of Me." The work of the Spirit includes witnessing to the work, words, power and glory of Jesus.

2) Guide into all truth: John 16:13 declares, "However, when He, the Spirit of truth, has come, He will guide you into all truth … ." Jesus also said that the Spirit does not "speak on His own authority, but whatever He hears He will speak." There is a total unity of our Lord God. The Holy Spirit will never lead anyone to do or say anything contrary to the Word of God, or contrary to the character, purpose, or plan of the Lord God revealed in Jesus. Notice Jesus said "all truth," not just biblical truths. All categories of truth are revealed to us by His Spirit. We learn as the Spirit of truth opens God's truth to us.

3) Helps us remember: "But the Helper, the Holy Spirit … will bring to your remembrance all things that I said to you" (John 14:26). The disciples could only absorb a certain amount of teaching. Jesus knew they would need help in the future remembering all that He had taught them. "He will glorify Me, for He will take of what is Mine and declare it to you" (John 16:14).

During the Vietnam War, some American prisoners of war were moved about in bamboo cages to keep them from being rescued. The POWs used every scrap of paper they could find and began writing down the Scripture verses they could remember and pass them around among themselves secretly. Later, when they were rescued, they testified of how those verses encouraged them and enabled them to survive the torture.

4) The world cannot receive: The world cannot know the Spirit (John 14:17), because the "world" stood for all those who did not believe in Jesus. They could not see Him or know Him. The disciples will know the Spirit because He dwells within them.

THE HOLY SPIRIT WILL NOT LEAVE A BELIEVER

In John 14:18, Jesus said: "I will not leave you orphans, I will come to you." The word "orphan" literally means "fatherless." An orphan in biblical times was a child with no father. Fathers in those days were the protectors, the providers, the spiritual leaders and teachers, and the teachers of a trade to their sons. A woman without a husband had few choices. They could go to their parents' home, or enter into a levirate marriage to one of her husband's relatives or depend on the benevolence of the people. Being an orphan was a serious situation. Jesus was going away, but He would not leave them as orphans. He said: "I will come to you" (John 14:18).

THE WORK OF THE SPIRIT IN THE WORLD

In John 16:5-11 is a summary of the work of the Spirit in the world. Jesus again explained that He was going away (John 16:5). Jesus' leaving was necessary so that the Helper could come (John 16:7). Jesus reassured His disciples that He would be with them: "And lo, I am with you always, even to the end of the age" (Matthew 28:20). Having assured the disciples of His presence with them, Jesus outlined what His Spirit would be doing in the world.

1) Convict the world of sin: The first work of the Holy Spirit in the world is to convict people of their sin (John 16:8). The word "convict" was used for the "cross-examination" of a witness or the person on trial. The idea of cross-examination was to "convince" a person they were wrong or to "convict" them of a crime. So the word carried both meanings: convict or convince.

Many of the Jews who wanted Jesus crucified probably thought they were serving God by eliminating a blasphemer who claimed to be the Son of God. But when Peter preached to them after the resurrection of Jesus found in Acts 2:37, the Jews were "pricked in their hearts." They were convicted of their sin and convinced that Jesus was the Messiah. That is the work of the Holy Spirit. You will never realize your need of a Savior until you are convicted of your sin (John 16:9).

2) Convince the world of righteousness: The second work of the Holy Spirit in the world is to convince people of righteousness (John 16:8). People must be convinced that Jesus is righteous. Jesus was crucified as a criminal. So why would people put their trust in a Jewish criminal who was crucified? That is the work of the Holy Spirit. The Holy Spirit convinces people that Jesus is righteous, that He arose from the dead, and ascended to His Father (John 16:10).

3) Convince the world of judgment: The third work of the Holy Spirit in the world is to convince people that there is a judgment. The judgment began on the cross. The ruler of this world, Satan, was judged and defeated (John 16:11). The Holy Spirit convinces people that there is a judgment coming for all people.

4) Convince the world of the need for salvation: This work of the Holy Spirit is not specifically mentioned here. However, when we are convicted of our sin (John 16:9), convinced of the righteousness of Jesus (John 16:10), convinced of coming judgment, and convinced our fatal sin is not believing in Jesus (John 16:9), then the next step is to repent of sin and trust Jesus as Lord and Savior.

The Holy Spirit is the presence of the Lord dwelling in believers and at work in our world. The question is: Do you have the Holy Spirit living in you? In Revelation 3:20, Jesus said: "Behold, I stand at the door and knock. If anyone hears My voice and opens the door, I will come in to him and dine with him, and he with Me."

Jesus is knocking. If "anyone" — that means you — will listen and open the door to your heart and life, Jesus will enter and dwell in you. That's the work of the Holy Spirit. Are you listening?

DAY 5, PART 8: 'FRIENDS OF JESUS' (JOHN 15:12-25)

Jesus had been instructing the disciples about two of the most wonderful gifts He would give them. One was complete, perfect joy. This gift of joy incorporated a gift of inner peace, security, and hope that came from knowing Jesus as Savior and Lord (John 15:11). The second wonderful gift that Jesus mentioned here is love: "[A]s I have loved you" (John 15:12). Jesus' love always seeks what is best for you. It is a selfless love. Jesus then began to explain the depths of this new love relationship that believers would have.

A LOVE RELATIONSHIP

Believers are commanded to "love one another" (John 15:12). That is not a suggestion. It is not: Love others if they are loveable. It is not: Love others if they are nice to you or agree with you. Love is a demand. Love is a verb. Love is something you do! Notice the character of this love. Jesus said: "[Y]ou love one another, as I have loved you" (John 15:12). Our love for others needs to be like Jesus' love for us!

At times, even in church, there is competition for position, disputes, quarrels and anger. These things should not be true in the church. Our churches would have a more dynamic impact on the lost world if they were seen living the loving example of Christ. "By this all will know that you are My disciples, if you have love for one another" (John 13:35).

Then Jesus gave the ultimate example of love: "Greater love has no one than this, than to lay down one's life for his friends" (John 15:13). That may be easy to say, but it is more difficult to have the depth of love where you are willing to die for someone else. The amazing grace of that statement is that Jesus not only commanded us to have His kind of love, He demonstrated that kind of love when He died on the cross.

This love relationship with Jesus is a bond that nothing can break. Paul wrote: "For I am persuaded that neither death nor life, nor angels nor principalities nor powers, nor things present nor things to come, nor height nor depth, nor any other created thing, shall be able to separate us from the love of God which is in Christ Jesus our Lord" (Romans 8:38-39).

Not Slaves, But Friends

Jesus said: "You are My friends, if you do whatever I command you" (John 15:14). Jesus no longer called them "servants" (John 15:15). The word translated "servant" literally is "slave." Being a "slave" of the Lord was not a title of shame in the Bible. Moses, (Deuteronomy 34:5), Joshua (Joshua 24:29), David (Psalm 89:20), Paul (Romans 1:1), James (1:1), Jude (1:1), Peter (2 Peter 1:1), and John (Revelation 1:1) were all "slaves" of the Lord.

But then Jesus called the disciples "friends" and no longer "slaves." A slave did not know what his master was doing. A slave was not consulted; he simply obeyed orders without being given an explanation. Jesus said you are friends, "for all things that I heard from My Father I have made known to you" (John 15:15).

In those days, slaves were simply human "tools." But believers are called to work with Jesus in sharing the gospel with others and growing the kingdom of God on this earth. Paul wrote: "For we are God's fellow workers ..." (1 Corinthians 3:9). We not only have the privilege of following the commands of our King, but also of working with Him. As friends of Jesus, the Holy Spirit dwells in us, and we are called to face the tremendous challenges of going into all the world with the gospel.

CALLED TO BE SENT OUT

The Great Commission (Matthew 28:20) challenges us to "go into all the world." Jesus also said: "As the Father has sent Me, I also send you" (John 20:21). Once we are saved, we have the mission of carrying the gospel wherever we go. Jesus said: "I have chosen you to send you out" (John 15:16). Jesus has not called you to just walk the church aisle, sit on the front pew, or walk into baptismal waters. He has called you to join His army. He has called you to be a "sent-out one" — a "missionary," who will proclaim Jesus as Lord to all people. Paul wrote: "We are ambassadors for Christ, as though God were pleading through us: we implore you on Christ's behalf, be reconciled to God" (2 Corinthians 5:20).

CALLED TO BEAR FRUIT

We are called to "bear fruit" (John 15:16). We are to be productive, not destructive, followers of Christ. We are "to bear fruit that will remain." It must be fruit that lasts. It is good to build church buildings, ministry centers, orphanages, Christian schools and Christian hospitals, but the real fruit is to build lives. Buildings are helpful, but the goal is to reach people for Christ. The real legacy of Pine Eden Church — or any church or ministry — is the redeemed, changed lives of people over the years. Lives changed for eternity are the real legacy of the church.

CALLED TO BE FAMILY

The command to love one another is found in verse 12 and verse 17. When we love one another, we are truly a family. Paul explained the concept well in Galatians 4:4-7: "But when the fullness of the time had come, God sent forth His Son, born of a woman, born under the law, to redeem those who were under the law, that we might receive the adoption as sons. And because you are sons, God has sent forth the Spirit of His Son into your hearts, crying out, 'Abba, Father!' Therefore you are no longer a slave but a son, and if a son, then an heir of God through Christ."

Jesus came to redeem the lost. The word "redeem" means to buy back a person from slavery. We are redeemed that "we might receive the adoption as sons" (Galatians 4:5). We have been given the Spirit into our hearts. "Therefore you are no longer a slave but a son, and if a son, then an heir of God through Christ" (Galatians 4:7).

EXPECT PERSECUTION

Being a part of the family of God doesn't mean that life will be easy. Life is difficult at best, and impossible without Jesus. The Lord did not prevent Shadrach, Meshach, and Abed-Nego from being thrown into the fiery furnace, but He was in the furnace with them (Daniel 3:25).

1) Jesus and His followers will be hated. Jesus said: "If the world hates you, you know that it hated me before it hated you" (John 15:18). For John, people were divided between those in the kingdom of God and those outside of it. When Jesus spoke of the "world," He was talking about people who were living their lives without faith in the Lord. That world is in opposition to the cause of Christ. There is no neutral ground. You are either on Jesus' side, or you aren't.

Legend has it that during General Santa Anna's siege of the Alamo, a remarkable event happened. With 5,000 trained troops surrounding an old mission in San Antonio turned into a fort by the Texans with 163 men inside, Santa Anna demanded their surrender. Colonel Travis stood in the courtyard and told his men that no help was coming, but he was going to stay and fight. He drew a line in the dirt with his sword. All who would stay and fight were to step across that line. They all did. They all died. But Texas, with the cry, "Remember the Alamo," won their independence. By the way, there were more Tennesseans in the Alamo than troops from any other state; among the most famous was Davy Crockett.

2) In New Testament times: The Roman government demanded that everyone pledge their support by declaring "Caesar is Lord." Christians would not call any man "Lord." Only Jesus is Lord! So Christians were seen as traitors. Christians will be hated, too (John 15:19).

Recently, a major league baseball player refused to kneel and hold a black piece of cloth during the playing of the national anthem before a game. Both teams did this except for one player. The teams said they were showing unity and supporting Black Lives Matter. This one player knew that Black Lives Matter was not just a slogan, but also, for some, may be associated with a Marxist organization that wants to destroy the nuclear family, is anti-Christian, and is anti-government. But his main reason for refusing was: "I am a Christian. I will not bow my knees to anyone but Jesus." He went on to explain that he had heard of the protest at the last minute and did not have time to explain his position ahead of time. What would you have done? Is Jesus really your Lord?

3) The "world" also hates believers and Jesus, because "they do not know Him who sent Me" (John 15:21). The world had heard Jesus' words (John 15:22) and seen His works (John 15:24); they have "no excuse for their sin" (John 15:22). The world hates Jesus and the Father (John 15:23-24).

When Jesus came, He exposed sin. Through His words and actions, Jesus made it clear that people needed to place their faith in Him. Jesus not only exposed sin and called us to follow Him, but His death on the cross also paid the penalty for sin. Now through the power of His Holy Spirit, He helps us overcome sin and inherit eternal life.

Who is lord of your life? Is it the things, the stuff of this world? To whom or what are you bowing your knees? Is Jesus Lord of your life?

DAY 5, PART 9: 'TRIBULATION AND COURAGE' (JOHN 16:1-4, 29-33)

Jesus predicted that persecution would come. Jesus wanted His disciples to be prepared, to know what was coming, and be willing to follow Him no matter what the cost. Jesus had made it clear that there was danger in following Him. Jesus had said: "If anyone desires to come after Me, let him deny himself, and take up his cross, and follow Me" (Matthew 16:24). To Jesus, the cross was not a decorative piece of jewelry, but a cruel instrument of death. What if Jesus asked you today: Will you take up your death row electric chair and follow Me? Jesus was asking His disciples to be willing to follow Him to their death.

NOT STUMBLE

By the time John wrote the Revelation, Roman persecution was a reality, in addition to persecution from the Jews. Jesus said: "Do not fear any of those things which you are about to suffer. Indeed, the devil is about to throw some of you into prison, that you may be tested, and you will have tribulation ten days. Be faithful until death, and I will give you the crown of life" (Revelation 2:10).

Jesus said: "These things I have spoken to you, that you should not be made to stumble" (John 16:1). Jesus was warning His disciples of coming persecution. He wanted them not to be caught off guard so they would not falter in their faith. At first the persecution would take two forms:

1) Excommunication: "They will put you out of the synagogues ..." (John 16:2). The synagogue was at the heart of the Jewish faith and community. If cast out of the synagogue, they would be ostracized from Jewish life and their family. They would be alone. This was a powerful tool of the orthodox Jews to keep people in line. If you stand for Christ today in the public arena, you may be standing alone. You may be the only one at your work, in your neighborhood, in your school, or on your team who will take a stand for biblical truth and morality in our increasingly godless society. You may find yourself alone. But you are never alone, for the Lord is with you. Jesus promised: "I will never leave you nor forsake you."

2) Death: "Yes, the time is coming that whoever kills you will think that he offers God service" (John 16:2). The word "service" was the word for the service a priest offered at the altar of the temple of the Lord in Jerusalem. It is the usual word for "religious service." Saul of Tarsus thought that he was serving God when he was trying to destroy the followers of Jesus: "Thus Saul, still breathing threats and murder against the disciples of the Lord ..." (Acts 9:1). And later in Paul's testimony before King Agrippa, he said: "Many of the saints I shut up in prison ... and when they were put to death, I cast my vote against them. And I punished them often in every synagogue and compelled them to blaspheme ... and being exceedingly enraged against them, I persecuted them even to foreign cities" (Acts 26:10-11).

Christians are dying for their faith around the world today. You may not face torture or death for your faith, but you may be ostracized or shunned or made fun of because of your faith.

WE BELIEVE

John closed out Chapter 16 on this same theme of persecution. The subject came up again when the disciples suddenly understood a great truth. "Now we are sure that You know all things ..." (John 16:30). The disciples earlier had been discussing among themselves the meaning of what Jesus had said (John 16:17-18). But then Jesus answered their questions without them asking Him (John 16:19). Jesus knew their minds. The disciples realized that Jesus knew all about them. Because

Jesus had told them about the Father and He also knew all about them, they were convinced that He was the Son of God (John 16:30).

Jesus knows your mind as well. There is nothing you can hide from the Lord. You may be able to fool most of the people most of the time, but you cannot hide anything from Jesus. Your life is an open book to Jesus. Jesus wants you to admit your sin, repent and turn in faith to Him.

The Hour Has Come

Although the disciples now believed that Jesus was truly the Son of God, Jesus knew His time had come for Him to pay the penalty for sin. Jesus told the disciples what they would do when the time came for the cross (John 16:32).

1) Scattered: They would all desert Him. Jesus knew their weaknesses. Yet Jesus still loved them and would entrust to them the work of the kingdom on earth when He ascended to His Father. Jesus was not alone, because, as Jesus said, "the Father is with Me" (John 16:32).

You and I are never alone, because the Holy Spirit is always dwelling in the life of believers. When you stand for biblical truth, when you stand up for Jesus, you are never alone. Jesus is a friend who never deserts you.

2) Forgiveness: Jesus knew what they would do, but He had already forgiven them. He did not belittle them, and later He did not hold their desertion against them. Jesus loved them in spite of their failures. Jesus loves you in spite of your failures. Jesus knows all about you, but He receives you just as you are, and forgives you and works in your life to help you grow to be the person He knows you can become.

The Promise of Peace in the Midst of Trouble

Knowing all the trouble ahead, Jesus offered to the disciples His peace: "These things I have spoken to you, that in Me you might have peace" (John 16:33). The word translated "peace" does not simply mean the absence of conflict. The word could also be translated "harmony, tranquility, safety, welfare, and health." The word "peace" was often used as a verbal greeting. This one word carries a list of items of goodwill spoken to another person. Jesus' use of this word shows that He was concerned about their total well-being. Jesus said: "My peace I leave with you, My peace I give to you" (John 14:27; 20:19, 21, 26).

TRIBULATION

Jesus warned His disciples that on this earth they would have tribulation (John 16:33). Since Jesus warned them ahead of time about tribulation and their desertion, when it happened they would not be in despair. Jesus expressed His love, forgiveness, and peace ahead of time.

It would make a tremendous difference in our relationships with others if we were less concerned about being hurt and more concerned about not hurting others. We should follow Jesus' example of love and thoughtfulness.

COURAGE

The Christian life does not guarantee that you will escape all trouble and heartache. In verse 33, Jesus made some of the most astounding statements ever contained in one verse:

1) *"In Me you have peace."*

2) *"In the world you have tribulation."*

3) *"Be of good cheer."*

The word "cheer" is literally "take heart." The expression came to mean "courage." In facing the problems and troubles ahead, believers can do so with courage. Why?

4) *"I have overcome the world."* The victory is already won. Although

there is tribulation in the world, there is peace and much more: There is victory in Jesus.

Are you standing in the winner's circle right now? You are if you have taken your stand with Jesus!

In our stressful, turbulent world, wouldn't you like to have peace? Wouldn't you like to have real harmony, tranquility, safety, welfare, and health? Then come to Jesus. Come to Jesus now.

DAY 5, PART 10: 'JESUS' PRAYER IN THE UPPER ROOM' (JOHN 17:1-26)

Jesus began His prayer by calling on His Father, knowing His hour had come (John 17:1). After this prayer, Jesus would go out to the Garden of Gethsemane and be betrayed by Judas, arrested, go through false trials and be crucified. It is important to realize that before these terrible events, Jesus prayed. He prayed for Himself, He prayed for His disciples, and He prayed for you!

JESUS PRAYED FOR HIMSELF

1) Jesus prayed: "Glorify Your Son, that Your Son also may glorify You" (John 17:1). Jesus' glory was the cross. The cross was Jesus' mission, and He was obediently going to the cross. Jesus said: "I have finished the work which You have given Me to do" (John 17:4). Jesus had committed Himself to the completion of the assignment of salvation given to Him by His Father. Jesus glorified the Father by showing the immeasurable love of God that was willing to die on a cross to pay the penalty for sin and provide eternal life to all who believe (John 17:2). Jesus glorified the Father by His perfect obedience, in perfect love by going to the cross.

But the cross was not the end. Jesus won the victory over sin, death, and hell through the resurrection. All glory, honor, and praise to our

Lord, who had conquered all that we might have life through His name. The cross had to be endured first before Jesus could return to the Father. Jesus came from the Father, made sacrifice for our sin, and returned to the Father (John 17:5). Our entrance into the kingdom of God, our entrance into our heavenly home must be through the cross of Jesus. Our repentance and faith in Jesus and what He accomplished for us on the cross is our way home to the Father.

2) *"... that they may know You, the only true God, and Jesus Christ whom You have sent" (John 17:3).* The idea of knowing God is a theme of the Old Testament. Habakkuk had a vision of the time when "the earth will be filled with the knowledge of the glory of the Lord" (Habakkuk 2:14). But what does it mean "to know the Lord"? In the Old Testament, the word "know" was used for the most intimate knowledge between husband and wife. For example: "Now Adam knew Eve his wife, and she conceived and bore Cain" (Genesis 4:1). True love between a man and a woman is an intimacy of heart, mind, and soul. They are "no longer two, but one flesh" (Genesis 2:24). So to know the Lord is not just intellectual knowledge of the facts or Scriptures about the Lord. It means to have an intimate, personal relationship with the Lord, the most intimate relationship in your life. If Jesus had not come, this intimacy with the Lord God would not have been possible.

A mission statement I have used in the churches I have pastored for the last forty years is: "To Know Christ and to Make Him Known." When you understand what "know" means, that is a concise statement that grasps the thrust and meaning of the Christian life.

3) *"I have manifested Your name" (John 17:6):* In the Bible, the "name" meant the whole nature and character of a person. Jesus revealed what the Father is like (John 17:7-8). Jesus also said: "He that hath seen Me, hath seen the Father (John 14:9). In the seven "I Am Who I Am" sayings of Jesus, He revealed the characteristics of the name

Yahweh. He is the Bread of Life, the Light of the world, the Door, the Good Shepherd, the Way, the Truth, the Life, the Resurrection and the Life, and the True Vine.

JESUS PRAYED FOR HIS DISCIPLES

Jesus did not pray for the world, but for His disciples (John 17:9). We must remember that the "world" stood for all people in the world who had organized their lives and had left God out. Jesus loved the world (John 3:16), and His plan was to send His disciples into the world in order to win those in the world to faith in Him (John 17:18).

1) "... keep through Your name" (John 17:11): The word translated "keep" means "to guard." The old English name for jail is a "keep." Jesus also prayed that "I kept them in Your name" (John 17:12). I believe this involves our spiritual protection that will continue until we stand before the throne. Jesus prayed that "You should keep (guard) them from the evil one" (John 17:15).

In verse 15, Jesus also said: "I do not pray that You should take them out of the world ... ." Christianity is not meant to be lived in a monastery. It is not escapism from our problems. We are not to escape the world, but to evangelize the world (John 17:18).

2) "... that they may be one as We are" (John 17:11): Jesus did not mean organizational unity. We will never organize our churches the same way. We will not all worship the Lord the same way. We may differ on some small points in our beliefs. But we should be united in our love for the Lord Jesus Christ and for one another. The danger is that we might love our organizational system, our creed, our ritual more than we love one another. The unity of heart can prove to the world the truth of our faith in Christ.

3) "... that they may have My joy fulfilled in themselves" (John 17:13): As we have discussed before, Jesus is not talking about "happiness" which depends upon happenings. The joy that Jesus gives is an inner sense of His presence, His love, and care that the world can never take from us.

4) *"... that they also may be sanctified by the truth"* *(John 17:19):* The word "sanctify" is often translated "holy," but the basic meaning is "different or separate." The word had two ideas in it. One was that a person was "separated or set apart" for a special service for the Lord. The Lord said of Jeremiah: "Before I formed you in the womb I knew you, before you were born I sanctified you ..." (Jeremiah 1:5). The second idea was that the Lord also equipped that person to carry out their assignment. When we place our lives in the Lord's hands, He will equip us for the service he has called us to do "for the equipping of the saints for the work of ministry, for the edifying of the body of Christ" (Ephesians 4:12).

JESUS PRAYED FOR YOU

Jesus prayed: "I do not pray for these alone, but also for those who will believe in Me through their word" (John 17:20). Jesus' prayer for you involved several things:

1) *Jesus prayed that we would believe their word of witness.* Remember it is "the will of God that none should perish, but that all should come in repentance." Jesus' desire is that we would all heed the testimony, the witness of His first disciples and respond in faith.

2) *Jesus prayed that "they all may be one, as You, Father, are in Me, and I in You ..." (John 17:21).* Jesus and the Father are one in heart, mind, and purpose. Their oneness was evident in the love and obedience of Jesus. Our oneness does not mean organizational unity (John 17:22). It should be a unity of heart, mind and purpose. Our oneness in love will be a witness to the world that they "may believe that you have sent Me ..." (John 17:21), and that they "may know that you have sent Me ..." (John 17:23).

3) Jesus prayed that they "may be with Me where I am" (John 17:24). Not only did Jesus pray that we would be with Him, but that we would "behold My glory which You have given Me, for You loved Me before the foundation of the world" (John 17:24).

4) Jesus prayed that "I have known You; and these have known that You sent Me" (John 17:25). The world, those living outside of faith in Jesus, do not know God. But Jesus had intimate knowledge of the Father: "And I have declared to them Your name ..." (John 17:26). Jesus had told His disciples who the Father is. Jesus' desire was that "the love with which You loved Me may be in them, and I in them" (John 17:26).

If you are not living in the presence of Jesus now, you will not be in His presence after death. Seek an intimate relationship with Jesus with all your heart and soul. Grow closer to Jesus in times of studying His Word, in times of prayer on your knees, and in times of serving and giving your testimony of His saving grace.

What a blessing to remember not only that Jesus prayed for you, but that He is still praying for you. "Therefore He is also able to save to the uttermost those who come to God through Him, since He always lives to make intercession for them." (Hebrews 7:25).

Day 5, Part 10: 'Jesus' Arrest and First Trial' (John 18:1-14, 19-23)

When Jesus had finished His last teaching and had prayed with His disciples, they all left the upper room. They would have gone out an eastern gate of the lower city, down the slope to the Kidron Valley and crossed the Brook Kidron (John 18:1). They started up the Mount of Olives and entered a garden.

THE LAMB OF GOD

In preparation for the Passover, lambs were dedicated and sacrificed in the temple, and their blood was poured out on the altar as an offering to the Lord. There was a channel cut in the stone from the altar down to the Brook Kidron so the blood could drain out. Josephus, an ancient Jewish historian, reported a few years after Jesus' time that there were 256,000 lambs sacrificed at Passover. So when Jesus and His disciples crossed the Brook Kidron, the blood of the lambs would have still been evident. Jesus is called the "Lamb" eleven times in the Book of Revelation. Paul wrote: "For indeed Christ, our Passover, was sacrificed for us" (1 Corinthians 5:7).

THE GARDEN

The Garden of Gethsemane would have been someone's privately owned grove of olive trees. Jesus and His disciples must have been given access to the garden by the owner. "Gethsemane" means "oil press." Apparently there was a press in the garden to extract the oil from the olives. There are still several very old olive trees on the hillside that date back almost to the time of Jesus. This garden would have been a quiet retreat for Jesus and His disciples, and they must have used it often when they were in Jerusalem. Judas knew about the garden and Jesus' apparent custom of going there to pray. Judas knew it would be an ideal time and place to arrest Jesus when He was away from the huge crowds that usually flocked to Him.

THE ARREST

I find it very interesting that the Jewish authorities literally sent an army to capture Jesus. Jesus had no army, and was an unarmed teacher-preacher-healer who had no history of violence or rebellion. Yet, John reported that "a detachment of troops, and officers from the chief priests and Pharisees, came there with lanterns, torches, and weapons" (John 18:3).

1) The word "detachment" could refer to "cohort," a Roman name for a group of soldiers that ranged between 800 and 1,000 soldiers. It would not have been unusual for such a large number to be in Jerusalem at Passover time, because that was a key time for the revolutionists to stir up trouble. Sometimes the word "cohort" was used for a smaller group from the main contingent, consisting of 200 soldiers. Even if it was this smaller number, it still was a major force to capture one man.

2) The "officers" would have been the temple police force. They kept order in the temple area. The Sanhedrin, the ruling body of the Jews, also had officers who carried out their orders. This armed force ("weapons") came with "lanterns and torches" (John 18:3). Passover occurred during a full moon, so the night would have been relatively bright. They must have assumed that they would have to search for Jesus in some dark hiding places.

During Passover time, the Roman army came to Jerusalem and stayed at the Tower of Antonio, which was near the temple. They made their presence known and were prepared for any trouble.

3) The courage of Jesus: Apparently believing they would have to search for Jesus, they must have been startled when Jesus boldly stepped forward and asked: "Whom are you seeking?" (John 18:4). They answered: "Jesus of Nazareth." Jesus said to them: "I am He" (John 18:5). Jesus not only acknowledged that He was the one they were seeking, He again claimed to be "I Am Who I Am"! Jesus identified Himself as *Yahweh*! They were startled and fell to the ground (John 18:6). John also noted that the betrayer Judas was with the army (John 8:5). In the face of all these armed enemies, Jesus was calm. He was in charge of the situation. Jesus asked again: "Whom are you seeking?" They said, "Jesus of Nazareth" (John 18:7).

Remember, always put your trust in Jesus, no matter what the circumstances are. Jesus is in control and He will ultimately bring all things in line with His will and purpose (Romans 8:28). Even then Jesus could have overpowered all of them. He could have called down legions of angels to battle the soldiers. But Jesus went to the cross obediently, to pay the penalty for sin, that you and I might be saved.

4) The protective care of Jesus: Jesus again told the soldiers and officers that He was the one they were seeking. But this time He added: "Therefore, if you seek Me, let these go their way" (John 18:8). Jesus was not concerned for His own safety, but He was concerned for His disciples. He wanted to protect them. This was a fulfillment of what Jesus had prayed earlier: "Of those you gave Me, I have lost none" (John 18:9, 17:12).

5) The obedience of Jesus: Then Peter, with great courage against impossible odds, drew his sword and struck the high priest's servant, a man named Malchus. Peter, not being a soldier, only cut off the servant's ear. Luke related that Jesus touched his ear and healed him (Luke 22:51). Jesus then commanded Peter to put up His sword and declared: "Shall I not drink the cup which My Father has given Me?" (John 18:11).

Jesus was determined to be obedient to His Father's will. You and I, as believers should be determined to do the will of our Heavenly Father. Jesus wanted His followers to understand that His kingdom would not be established by force. People cannot be forced into becoming real believers. As the grace of God works on the human heart and mind, a person must choose to repent, trust Jesus, and follow Him.

THE TRIAL BEFORE ANNAS

The army, apparently all around Jesus, arrested Him and bound Him (John 18:12). The Jewish authorities must have been afraid of Jesus' power because they sent such a large force to arrest Him. They led

Jesus to the house of Annas in the night. Annas was not the high priest, his son-in-law Caiaphas was the high priest (John 18:13). John then reminded His readers that it was Caiaphas who had remarked: "That it was expedient that one man should die for the people" (John 18:14). He meant that it was better for Jesus to die than for the Romans to destroy their nation. John realized the true meaning was that Jesus was going to die so all people could be saved.

1) *This trial was illegal* because Annas was not the current high priest. The office of high priest was originally for life, but when the Romans conquered the Jews, the office went to the highest bidder. Through bribery, Annas had served as high priest from AD 6 to 15. Then four of his sons had been high priest. Annas' son-in-law Caiaphas was the present high priest.

2) *This trial was illegal* because it was held in the night. All trials were to be held in the daytime with the public invited to attend.

3) *This trial was illegal* because it was held in a private home and not the meeting place of the Sanhedrin.

4) *This trial was illegal* because by Jewish law, the accused could not be asked any questions in which, by answering, they might incriminate themselves. Annas questioned Jesus (John 18:19). Jesus responded that He had taught openly in the synagogues and in the temple. Jesus had taught publicly and had held no secret meetings where He taught anything contrary to His public teaching (John 18:20). So why not question the people? Call your witnesses, Jesus was basically saying (John 18:21).

5) *This trial was illegal* because by Jewish law, the accused had to have at least two witnesses who agreed to the charges brought against someone. There were not any witnesses.

6) *The trial was illegal* because Jesus was struck (John 18:22). The accused was not to be handled in this way. "Jesus answered him, 'If I

have spoken evil, bear witness of the evil; but if well, why do you strike Me?'" (John 18:23).

7) These proceedings were illegal because Jesus was considered guilty before He was tried. For example, back in John 11:53 and 57, John wrote: "Then, from that day on, they plotted to put Him to death"; and "Now both the chief priests and the Pharisees had given a command, that if anyone knew where He was, he should report it, that they might seize Him."

How many times have you judged someone's character based on gossip, before you knew the truth about them? If you have, you could be a Pharisee. How many times have you excused your sinful lifestyle by saying things like "Everybody is doing it," or "What harm is there in doing that?" or "There is no law against it!" If you have, you could be a Pharisee.

Today, if Christians stand upon the biblical standards of right and wrong, they are called a bigot or accused of "hate speech." When Jesus told the woman caught in the act of adultery "Go and sin no more" (John 8:11), was that hate speech? Or was Jesus offering her another chance to live a godly life? It is not hate speech to call evil, evil — or sin, sin. What would be hateful is to label a person for what they are and then not telling them about the love and forgiveness of Jesus Christ.

DAY 6: 'PETER'S DENIAL AND THE TRIAL BEFORE CAIAPHAS' (JOHN 18:15-18, 25-27)

The other disciples deserted Jesus when He was arrested, but Peter followed Jesus. After the trial before Annas, Jesus was taken to the home of the high priest Caiaphas. The Sanhedrin, the ruling body of the Jews, was assembled there (John 18:24).

Peter was following and came to the house of Caiaphas (John 18:15). This was probably after midnight, so it was day six or Friday. Another disciple was with Peter who knew the high priest, and he was able to enter the courtyard of Caiaphas' house (John 18:15). But Peter was on the outside. The disciple, who was known to the high priest, persuaded the female doorkeeper to allow Peter to come in (John 18:16).

This unnamed disciple quite possibly was John. John's family had a thriving fishing business. His father had hired servants (Mark 1:20). Fish were preserved by salting, so they could be transported. John may have delivered salted fish to the high priest's home in the past. So the doorkeeper and John may have been acquainted. We can't be certain about this, but John usually identified disciples by name, except when talking about himself. Peter wanted to be close to Jesus. Peter loved Jesus and did not want to abandon Him.

PETER

1) Peter's courage: Only Peter had the courage to draw his sword in the face of incredible odds to defend Jesus (John 18:10). All the other disciples fled when Jesus was arrested, except for Peter and the unnamed disciple. Peter would fail soon, but he dared to do more and go farther than any of the other disciples.

2) Peter's first denial: The servant girl who opened the door suspected that Peter was one of Jesus' disciples (John 18:17). Perhaps she had seen Jesus and the disciples during Jesus' public ministry in Jerusalem. Peter instantly denied it and said: "I am not" (John 18:17).

3) Peter's second denial: Later, as Peter stood and warmed himself by the fire, he was questioned again. Others were gathered around the fire while the Sanhedrin was sitting in judgment of Jesus. They said to Peter: "You are not also one of His disciples, are you?" Peter more forcefully denied it again and said: "I am not" (John 18:25).

4) Peter's third denial: Then one of the high priest's servants, who was a relative of Malchus, whose ear Peter had cut off, said: "Did I not see you in the garden with Him?" (John 18:26). Peter denied it again, "and immediately a rooster crowed" (John 18:27). I believe Peter must have instantly remembered what Jesus had said. Jesus had told Peter that before the rooster crowed he would deny Him three times (John 13:38).

Peter had thought he would remain faithful, but in his human weakness — and in a very stressful situation — Peter had denied his Lord. As a believer, you have made a commitment that none of us could keep without the presence of the Holy Spirit in our lives. If we keep our focus on Jesus and are aware of His presence through prayer, we can be faithful. But as followers of Christ, we are redeemed sinners. At times, like Paul, we might say: "For the good that I will to do, I do not do; but the evil I will not to do, that I practice" (Romans 7:19). Then Paul went on: "O wretched man that I am! Who will deliver me from this body of death?" (Romans 7:24). Then Paul declared the answer: "I thank God — through Jesus Christ our Lord!" (Romans 7:25).

In our human weakness, we all fail. But through repentance, our Lord is ready to forgive and restore us. In Jesus, failures are never final. In Jesus, sin is not the victor. In Jesus, the grave is not the goal. In Jesus, our hope is eternal.

Remember, Jesus said: "I have overcome the world"! (John 16:33). There is victory only in Jesus. When your whole world seems to be crumbling, if you are standing with Jesus, you will have the victory. When all others are fearful because of the problems we face, if you are standing with Jesus, you will have peace.

THE TRIAL BEFORE CAIAPHAS

John is silent about the events in the illegal trial before Caiaphas and the Sanhedrin. The other three gospels — beginning in Matthew 26:57, Mark 14:53, and Luke 22:63 — give some information about the trial in Caiaphas' house.

This trial was held at night; it was in Caiaphas' house; no witnesses could agree; Caiaphas resorted to questioning Jesus; they beat Jesus. All of these things were illegal according to Jewish law. Finally, they accused Jesus of blasphemy for claiming to be the Son of God.

Think to what lengths of lying and deception these religious leaders had to go to convict Jesus. They justified all of this to preserve their religion and position of power.

What lengths would you go to in order to protect your lifestyle? What would you resort to in order to justify what you say and do? Would you resort to gossip, lies or deception in order to maintain your position?

DAY 6, PART 2: 'THE TRIAL BEFORE PILATE' (JOHN 18:28-19:16)

The Sanhedrin had no legal right to execute anyone, because the Romans reserved that right for themselves. The Jewish method of execution had been stoning. The Jewish leaders wanted to publicly humiliate and discredit Jesus by having Him crucified as a common criminal. For that, they needed the Romans. It was about daylight. So they brought Jesus to the Roman governor, Pilate (John 18:28). Several times during the trial process, Pilate sought to release Jesus, but the Jews were adamant that Jesus be crucified. Jesus had said: "And I, if I be lifted up, will draw all men unto Me" (John 12:32). Jesus knew He would be lifted up on a cross and not stoned to death.

The Jews came early because they knew Pilate liked to carry out his official duties early, before the heat of the day. He usually headquartered in Caesarea on the Mediterranean coast. He was only in Jerusalem on special occasions like Passover.

PILATE'S FIRST RULING

The Jews would not enter the Praetorium because they would be defiled. A Jew would be ceremonially unclean if they entered a Gentile home or building. They wanted to avoid defilement in order to celebrate Passover (John 18:28). The Jews very carefully followed their ritual and ceremonial rules, but considered it proper to lie about Jesus, to hate Him, and want Him to be killed. Jesus had said: "Woe to you, scribes and Pharisees, hypocrites! For you pay the tithe of mint and anise and cummin, and have neglected the weightier matters of the law: justice and mercy and faith. These you ought to have done, without leaving the other undone" (Matthew 23:23).

So Pilate went outside to speak with the Jews and asked: "What accusation do you bring against this man?" (John 18:29). The Jews responded with an evasive statement that if Jesus was not an evildoer they would not have brought Him to Pilate (John 18:30).

Pilate sensed that this was a religious dispute, and he tried to avoid the situation. So Pilate's first ruling was: "You take Him and judge Him according to your law" (John 18:31). The Jews then made it very plain that they were seeking the death penalty (John 18:31). This would fulfill the saying of Jesus about being "lifted up" (John 18:32).

PILATE'S SECOND RULING

At this point, the Jews realized a religious charge of blasphemy would not work, so they told Pilate that Jesus called Himself a king. That would portray Jesus as a traitor and troublemaker for Rome. So Pilate reentered the Praetorium and asked Jesus: "Are You the King of the Jews?" (John 18:33). Jesus' answer was in the form of a question: Had Pilate arrived at this conclusion, or was this the accusation of the Jews? (John 18:34).

Pilate showed his disdain for the Jews by declaring: "Am I a Jew?" Then, basically, Pilate said to Jesus, "Your own people have brought this charge against you. Answer for yourself. What have you done?" (John 18:35).

Jesus explained to Pilate that His kingdom was not of this world. Jesus did not rule as a king over an earthly domain. If Jesus had an earthly kingdom, His followers would fight to prevent His arrest. (John 18:36). Pilate responded: "Are You a king then?" Jesus responded that He was a king. But He was born into this world to bear witness to the truth. All those who are true respond to Jesus' voice (John 18:37). Jesus' kingdom is a spiritual kingdom, but Pilate did not grasp that concept. He replied perhaps with a sarcastic tone or a discouraged, disillusioned tone: "What is truth?"

Then Pilate rendered his second ruling: "I find no fault in Him at all" (John 18:38). According to Roman law, this is the exact wording of an official verdict in a Roman court of law. The case should have been closed at that point.

PILATE'S THIRD RULING

According to Luke's gospel, it was at this point that Pilate realized that Jesus was from Galilee (Luke 23:6). So Pilate sent Jesus to Herod, who had the jurisdiction of Galilee and was also in Jerusalem at that time. Herod was glad to see Jesus because he hoped to see some miracle. Herod questioned Jesus, but Jesus was silent. The chief priests and scribes were present, vehemently accusing Jesus. Herod's guard treated Jesus with contempt, and mocked Him and sent Him back to Pilate (Luke 23:7-12).

PILATE'S FOURTH RULING

In an effort to release Jesus, whom he had ruled to be innocent, Pilate did not have the courage to stand up to this angry mob, so he tried to find a way to release Jesus without causing a riot (John 18:39). "Do you want me to release to you the King of the Jews?" Pilate asked (John 18:39). The crowd shouted, "Not this Man, but Barabbas!" Now

Barabbas was an insurrectionist and a murderer (Matthew 27:15-26; Mark 15:6-15; and Luke 23:17-25). He was probably devoted to the cause of freeing Israel from the Romans and became involved in robbery and murder. Because of his fight against the Romans, he must have been popular with the people.

The choice of the mob has always been force and violence. So they picked the violent man, Barabbas, instead of Jesus, who came in love and peace. Our nation was torn in the summer of 2020 with some of the worst domestic violence in our history. The mob rules in the streets of many cities in America. Human nature, without faith in Jesus, descend into sin and violence.

PILATE'S FIFTH RULING

Pilate's next move was to severely punish Jesus, perhaps with the idea that this might appease the Jews. "So then Pilate took Jesus and scourged Him" (John 19:1). The object of scourging was to bring a person as close to death as possible. Two soldiers, one on either side, administered the scourging. The whip had a wooden handle with six braided leather strips attached. At the end of the strips were tied pieces of sharp bone or lead. The victims were tied to a stake. A person was beaten from their shoulder to their knees. The lashes would bruise and then cut the skin. The pieces of bone and lead would cut into the skin and muscle and rip it away when the lash was pulled back. The beating would cut into the muscles, leaving strips of bleeding flesh. The loss of blood would be great. Victims usually passed out in a few minutes. Often organs were exposed and slashed. Many died from the beating. Jesus survived the beating, but later He was so weak, He was not able to carry His cross (Mark 15:21).

Pilate's Sixth Ruling

When Jesus came out, perhaps Pilate thought the bloodthirsty Jews would be satisfied. Jesus was wearing the crown of thorns and the purple robe. Jesus would have been covered with blood. Pilate shouted: "Behold the Man!" (John 19:5). But "when the chief priests and officers saw Him, they cried out, saying, 'Crucify Him, crucify Him!'" (John 19:6). Pilate, in apparent frustration replied: "You take Him and crucify Him, for I find no fault in Him" (John 19:6).

The Jews then returned to their religious charge and answered that according to their law, He ought to die, "because He said He was the Son of God" (John 19:7). Pilate was frightened when he heard that (John 19:8). So Pilate questioned Jesus again and asked: "Where are you from?" (John 19:9). Jesus was silent. Pilate commanded Jesus to speak, explaining he had the power of life and death (John 19:10). Jesus responded that Pilate could have no authority over Him, unless God had granted it (John 19:11).

Pilate, all the more, wanted to release Jesus, but the mob cried out that if Pilate let Jesus go, he was not Caesar's friend. That was a technical term that meant you were a loyal supporter of Caesar. Of course, if you were not, you could be put to death. Since Jesus claimed to be a king, releasing Jesus would put Pilate in a dangerous position (John 19:12).

Pilate's Seventh Ruling

Pilate brought Jesus out, and Pilate took his place on the judgment seat (John 19:13). John pointed out that it was the sixth hour and the Preparation Day right before the Sabbath of Passover (John 19:14). But when the mob saw Jesus, "They cried out, away with Him, away with Him!" Pilate asked them: "Shall I crucify your King?" The chief priests answered, "We have no king but Caesar!" (John 19:15). What a shocking statement! The Lord God was supposed to be the only king over Israel.

But now the religious leaders were willing to declare that Caesar was king in order to crucify Jesus. In their anger, they totally renounced God in order to get their way.

So many people today have turned their backs on the Lord God in order to get their own way. So Pilate gave his final verdict and cowardly gave the mob permission to crucify Jesus (John 19:16).

1) *The Jews had become a bloodthirsty mob, with no regard for God or God's ways.* Does that sound familiar? Don't run with the crowd unless they are running to Jesus! The Jews ignored all of their own rules of justice to crucify an innocent man. When you are angry, do you ignore Jesus and the Christian rules of morality and love?

2) *Pilate was a coward.* He was afraid of losing his position. He was afraid of being reported if he let Jesus go, and he was afraid of the angry mob. Jesus told His disciples: "Fear not." When we follow Jesus, we don't have to be afraid.

3) *The Roman soldiers were following orders.* Then they added the mockery of Jesus as a king. They seemed to enjoy brutalizing Jesus. Have you become so accustomed to violence and a lack of morals in America that it doesn't bother you anymore? Do you blindly follow what others tell you to do, without consulting Jesus or His Word? We can so easily be caught up in the mob mentality of our day that we lose sight of the One who really matters — the Lord Jesus Christ.

Day 6, Part 3: 'The King On a Cross' (John 19:17-20)

The King

1) *Pilate's charge against Jesus, the soldiers' mockery, and the sign nailed to the cross above Jesus' head all proclaimed Him as King.* The charge against a criminal to be executed was written on a board. The charge against Jesus

was: "Jesus of Nazareth, the King of the Jews" (John 19:19). The board was carried in the procession as they wound through the narrow and twisting streets that became known as the *Via Dolorosa,* or "Way of Sorrows."

2) *Jesus was paraded through the streets so as many people as possible might see what would happen to anyone who dared to oppose Roman rule.* The victim had to carry his own cross that could weigh as much as 200 pounds. Because of the scourging, Jesus fell under the weight. The other three gospels wrote that a person in the crowd, Simon of Cyrene, was forced by the Romans to carry Jesus' cross.

3) *The place of crucifixion was outside the city, according to Mosaic law (Numbers 15:35).* It was at a crossroads, where many people would see it as they passed by. The writing on Jesus' placard was in Hebrew, Greek, and Latin (John 19:20), so all who passed by could read the crime for which Jesus was executed.

4) *When Pilate had questioned Jesus about being a king, Jesus said: "My kingdom is not of this world" (John 18:36).* Later, Jesus said: "You say rightly that I am a king ..." (John 18:37).

Jesus was beaten, spat upon, and nailed to a cross and died that you and I might live. The cross of Jesus today gives all people hope, if they will accept Jesus as their King. This hope could not be stopped by a cross. Jesus is alive and He is the King of kings and the Lord of lords.

CRUCIFIXION

1) *Crucifixion was a common sight in Jesus' time.* Victims were forced to carry their own cross to the place of execution. We know Jesus fell under the weight of the cross because of the scourging. Jesus was executed at a "place called the Place of a Skull, which is called in Hebrew, Golgotha" (John 19:17). Some have thought this meant a place where dead bodies were exposed, but the Jews would never have allowed that to happen. After bodies had decomposed in a tomb, the bones were placed in a stone

box called an ossuary and left in the tomb. There is a hill, which is a short distance from Jerusalem's northern gate, that has the appearance of a skull that is called today "Gordon's Calvary." There is a nearby garden with a tomb. No one knows for certain where Jesus' tomb was located, but this site gives a person an idea of what the area would have looked like.

2) Crucifixion was designed to cause the maximum pain. "Golgotha, where they crucified Him ..." (John 19:18). This form of execution was used only for non-Romans, slaves, rebels, and the worst criminals. Jesus would have been laid on the cross as it lay flat on the ground. With two soldiers holding down one of Jesus' arms, another soldier drove a spike through the wrist, at the heel of the hand. A nail through the palm of the hand would not support the weight of the body. Driving the nail at this point would have aggravated the median nerve.

3) The spikes they used were square in shape, about five and a half inches long and about a third of an inch across the top. The nailing of Jesus' hand would have caused His thumb and fingers to cramp inward.

4) The soldiers would then take Jesus' legs and place the right foot over the left, bend His knees upward at a twenty-degree angle, and then they drove a spike through the second metatarsal space of the feet. This spike injured the peroneal nerve and the medial and lateral plantar nerves. The membrane with nerves and blood vessels that surround the bones of the feet would be penetrated, causing intense pain.

5) The cross would then have been lifted up and dropped into a hole in the ground. The jolt would have sent pain all through Jesus' body. The weight of His body would have caused Jesus to be in a slumped down position. The weight of His body would enable the breathing muscle to inhale, but not exhale. The usual cause of death was asphyxiation and loss of blood. I read many years ago what Dr. Thurman Davis wrote about the medical effects of crucifixion.

6) As Jesus hung there, unable to breathe, tetany — a condition marked by cramps — would set in. Tetany was caused by the lack of oxygen and the inability to exhale carbon dioxide. In order to breathe, Jesus would have to push on His nailed feet, and pull up with His nailed hands, to move upward. Every movement would have torn at His shredded back against the wooden cross. Each time Jesus spoke from the cross, He had to do this.

7) Jesus suffered for hours from terrible pain, cramps, partial suffocation, and bleeding from His wounds. Then another agony began: a deep, crushing pain in the chest as the pericardium filled with serum and began to compress His heart. With all of this happening, Jesus showed His strength by speaking from the cross seven times!

Jesus Had Warned the Disciples

Jesus had told His disciples about His coming suffering and death many times (John 12:32, for example). The Messiah's death had been predicted by Isaiah and other prophets hundreds of years before. The Messiah would be "despised and rejected by men, a Man of sorrows and acquainted with grief … surely He has borne our griefs and carried our sorrows … He was wounded for our transgressions, He was bruised for our iniquities … by His stripes we are healed. All we like sheep have gone astray; we have turned, everyone, to his own way; and the Lord has laid on Him the iniquity of us all" (Isaiah 53:3-6).

Jesus' Death Was God's Plan for Redemption

The worst part of Jesus' suffering on the cross was that God "made Him who knew no sin to be sin for us, that we might become the righteousness of God in Him" (2 Corinthians 5:21). This was God's plan to redeem sinful people, who would believe and follow Jesus. God's story of redemption through the Bible led to the cross of Jesus Christ. Jesus' death paid the penalty for sin.

DAY 6, PART 4: 'JESUS PAID IT ALL'
(JOHN 19:21-41)

PILATE REFUSED TO CHANGE THE SIGN

The leaders of the Jews, the chief priests, went to Pilate. Friday was the Preparation Day for the Sabbath, and this was a special Sabbath because it came at Passover. They were not worried about being defiled by being in the presence of this Gentile, even during these holy days. They wanted the message on Jesus' sign changed. They did not want the sign on the cross to read, "King of the Jews," but that Jesus had said, "I am the King of the Jews" (John 19:21).

For the first time in the whole trial before Pilate, he took a strong stand and did not give in to the Jewish leaders. Pilate said: "What I have written, I have written." Pilate refused to change the sign (John 19:22). Jesus' crime was considered the most serious. That is why Jesus' cross was in the middle of the three who were crucified that day (John 19:18).

Will you have the courage to stand up for Jesus? There are so many people today in the media, the entertainment world, sports, politics, and the general public that seem determined to create a society that excludes God. Will you take a stand for Jesus?

THE SOLDIERS

After the soldiers had completed their assignment of nailing Jesus to the cross, they began to very casually divide Jesus' garments among them. Clothing was valuable in those days. The soldiers might have kept the clothing for themselves or sold it to profit by Jesus' death (John 19:23). Since the tunic was woven in one piece, the soldiers decided to cast lots to see who would have it, instead of tearing it into equal parts (John 19:24). This was another fulfillment of Scripture (Psalm 22:18).

You are gambling away your soul when you are indifferent to the cross of Christ. Ignoring Jesus' death on the cross will lead you into eternal darkness. The soldiers were very near Jesus on the cross. You may be near Christians, or live near a church, but still miss Jesus. You may be only the step of faith away. Trust Jesus. Trust Him now.

'BEHOLD, YOUR MOTHER'

John wrote that Mary, Jesus' mother, was standing near the cross. She may not have understood all that was happening, but she still had a mother's love for her Son. The sister of Jesus' mother was there. Looking at the parallel passages in Matthew 27:56 and Mark 15:40, her name was Salome, the mother of James and John. Mary, the wife of Clopas — about whom we know nothing else — was there. Also, Mary Magdalene was there with them (John 19:25). Jesus had cast seven demons out of her, and she had become a devoted follower (Mark 16:9).

When Jesus saw His mother, in spite of all the agony of the cross, He had concern for her. Jesus was Mary's eldest son, and apparently Joseph was dead. Jesus was thinking more of His mother's sorrow than of His own distress. Jesus also saw "the disciple whom He loved" (John) standing there. So Jesus made the tremendous effort to push Himself up, gulp some air and speak: "Woman, behold your son!" (John 19:26). To the disciple, Jesus said: "Behold your mother!" From that time on, John cared for Mary (John 19:27).

'I THIRST'

John records that later Jesus spoke again, saying: "I thirst" (John 19:28). Being thirsty showed Jesus' human nature. Jesus was fully human and fully God. One of the terrible consequences of crucifixion, due to sluggish blood flow and exposure, was a burning thirst. The sour wine on a sponge was lifted up to Jesus' lips as a way to ease His thirst.

When John was writing his gospel, there was a teaching that the spirit was good, but all physical matter was evil. This teaching was called Gnosticism. When this teaching came into the early church, some thought that Jesus could not have been human, but must have always been a spirit. John made it clear in his gospel that Jesus is the Son of God, and yet He came as a man to redeem the lost (John 1:1, 1:14).

IT IS FINISHED

The phrase translated "It is finished" comes from a Greek word, *tetelestai.* When we pay a bill in person today, often the statement is stamped "paid" or "paid in full." In Jesus' time, when someone paid a debt, the word *tetelestai* would be written to signify that the debt was "paid in full" (John 19:30). Jesus said from the cross that our sin debt was "paid in full." The ransom for our sin debt was paid in full when Jesus died on the cross. All the sacrifice that the Father had required for the sin of the world had been paid in full by Jesus. Paul wrote: "For you were bought at a price; therefore glorify God in your body and in your spirit, which are God's" (1 Corinthians 6:20). Yes, "Jesus paid it all, all to Him I owe" (from the hymn by Elvina M. Hall).

When Jesus said that, He bowed His head and "gave up His Spirit" (John 19:30). No one took Jesus' life from Him. Jesus willingly and obediently went to the cross to fulfill His Father's plan. The perfect Son of God was the only One who would be the perfect sacrifice for the sin of the world. Even at the point of death, Jesus was still in control. He surrendered His Spirit. Luke recorded that Jesus said: "Father, into Your hands I commit My spirit" (Luke 23:46). Jesus knew where He came from and where He was going. Jesus went through all of this for you and for the whole world.

JESUS' SIDE IS PIERCED

The Jews did not want the bodies to stay exposed on the crosses on the Sabbath — especially since this was a special Passover Sabbath (John 19:31). Again, the Jews broke their own rules by going to Pilate.

In order to hasten death, the victim's legs were broken. They then would not be able to push themselves up to breathe, and death would soon follow. So the soldiers came and the legs of the two criminals on both sides of Jesus were broken (John 19:32). But Jesus was already dead, so they did not break His legs (John 19:33). This was to fulfill the Scriptures concerning the instructions for preparing the Passover lamb by Moses when the Israelites were in Egypt (Exodus 12:46, Numbers 9:12, John 19:36). Paul wrote in 1 Corinthians 5:7: "For indeed Christ, our Passover, was sacrificed for us." John the Baptist said while pointing to Jesus: "Behold! The Lamb of God who takes away the sin of the world!" (John 1:29).

Then one of the soldiers pierced Jesus' side with his spear and blood, and water came out (John 19:34). This was probably the blood and fluid from the pericardium around Jesus' heart. This fulfilled the prophecy of Zechariah 12:10: "They shall look on Him whom they pierced" (John 19:37).

John's Testimony

John said that he had seen these things happen and that he was telling the truth: "so that you may believe" (John 19:35). The reason for John writing his gospel was so "that you may believe that Jesus is the Christ, the Son of God, and that believing, you may have life in His name" (John 20:31).

Do you believe that Jesus is the Christ, the Son of God?

The Burial of Jesus

Joseph of Arimathea, a wealthy member of the Sanhedrin and a secret disciple of Jesus for fear of the Jews, boldly went to Pilate and asked Pilate for permission to take the body of Jesus (John 19:38). Nicodemus was also a member of the Sanhedrin and a secret disciple of Jesus. They were either absent or silent when Jesus was tried before Caiaphas and the Sanhedrin. But after Jesus died on the cross, they were both emboldened to go public with their devotion to Jesus. Nicodemus brought spices for Jesus' burial. He brought a hundred pounds of myrrh and aloes (John 19:39). This was an expensive and kind gesture. The Jews wrapped bodies in linen strips with spices all mixed in (John 19:40).

Now in the place where Jesus was crucified, there was a garden and a new tomb that had never been used (John 19:41). Jesus was placed in that tomb because time was short because of the Jews' Preparation Day, and the tomb was nearby (John 19:42). Since the Jewish day began at 6 p.m., Jesus was in the tomb before 6 p.m. on Friday.

The cross of Jesus was already drawing people to Jesus. Two very prominent and influential people, Joseph and Nicodemus, had already responded openly after Jesus died on the cross. Jesus had said: "And I, if I be lifted up from the earth, will draw all people unto Myself" (John 12:32). They were already coming.

CHAPTER 7

THE 7 RESURRECTION EVENTS

EVENT 1: 'MARY AT THE EMPTY TOMB' (JOHN 20:1-2, 11-18)

Mary Magdalene had been a devoted follower of Jesus ever since He cast seven demons out of her (Mark 16:9). Mary Magdalene had also been at the cross (John 19:25). She had watched as Joseph of Arimathea placed Jesus' body in the tomb (Matthew 27:61). Then on the first day of the week, Sunday, Mary Magdalene went early to the tomb. The word translated "early" is the word for the fourth watch of the night, which was from 3 to 6 a.m. Mary came "while it was still dark" (John 20:1).

MARY AT THE TOMB

When Mary Magdalene came to the tomb, the stone was rolled away. Tombs in ancient times in Israel were cave-like structures carved out of the hillside. In front of the entrance was a groove in the ground. A large circular stone was placed in that groove and rolled to cover the entrance. The Jews had appealed to Pilate to seal the stone and place a guard to make sure the stone would not be moved (Matthew 27:66).

When Mary came to the tomb, the stone was rolled away and she realized Jesus' body was gone. We do not know what all she thought about this, but we know that she immediately started running to tell the disciples. Think how disturbed she must have been to run. It would have been very difficult to run in the long robes women wore. The only disciples she encountered were Peter and John. She told them: "They have taken the Lord out of the tomb, and we do not know where they have laid Him" (John 20:2). That statement reveals that Mary had no conviction that Jesus was resurrected. She thought that someone, for some reason, had moved Jesus' body.

MARY MET TWO ANGELS

While Peter and John ran on ahead, Mary returned to the tomb. Peter and John had already left. Mary was outside the tomb weeping. She stooped down and looked into the tomb (John 20:11). Mary saw two angels sitting in the tomb, one where Jesus' head had been and the other where His feet had been (John 20:12). The angels asked Mary: "Woman, why are you weeping?" She gave them the same explanation that she had given to Peter and John: "Because they have taken away my Lord, and I do not know where they have laid Him" (John 20:13).

When Mary had made a similar statement to Peter and John, Mary had said "the Lord" (John 20:2). That statement showed that Mary believed Jesus to be the Christ, the Son of God. In verse 13, Mary said "my Lord." It is good to believe that Jesus is the Lord. But real commitment to Jesus begins when you have experienced forgiveness, redemption, and restoration from Jesus, and you can testify that Jesus is "my Lord."

MARY MET THE MASTER

Then Mary turned around and saw Jesus, but did not recognized Him. Why not?

1) She thought He was dead. She did not yet believe in the resurrection and did not expect to see Jesus alive. What do you expect when you attend a worship service? If you come with an open, seeking heart, in a spirit of repentance and praise, you will feel the presence of the Lord. If you are expecting to attend just another meeting, that's probably what it will be for you.

2) Mary's tears could have blinded her eyes. In her sorrow and sense of loss her focus, her full attention was not on this stranger who spoke to her. She couldn't see Jesus because of her tears.

3) Mary was looking in the wrong direction. The Scriptures tell us that Mary turned and saw Jesus but did not know Him (John 20:14). Then Jesus said: "Woman, why are you weeping? Whom are you seeking?" Mary thought He was the gardener and said: "Sir, if you have carried Him away, tell me where you have laid Him, and I will take Him away." (John 20:15). Mary must have had her face turned away from Jesus because when He said her name, "she turned and said to Him, 'Rabboni'!" (John 20:16). John explained to his Greek readers that the term *rabboni* meant teacher. There was the familiar way Jesus spoke her name, and she turned and realized it was Jesus.

There are times when Jesus is calling us to meet a specific need — to help a certain person. But we are too busy looking in the other direction. Our focus may be on the concerns or things of the world and not on Jesus. So we miss His call, we miss the opportunity to be a fellow-laborer with the Lord Jesus. Where is your focus?

JESUS' COMMANDS FOR MARY

1) "Do not cling to Me ..." (John 20:17): Mary had apparently held Jesus by the feet and worshipped Him (see Matthew 28:9). Jesus commanded Mary Magdalene to stop clinging to Him. Jesus would soon be going back to His Father, but now she had to go and tell "My brethren and say to them, 'I am ascending to My Father and your Father, and to My God and your God'" (John 20:17).

2) "Go and tell": Jesus gave Mary an assignment. It was urgent. Time was short. Go! Tell! Others need to hear the good news from the graveyard. Jesus is alive!

3) Jesus' new relationship with His followers: Jesus commanded Mary to go and tell "My brethren." They were His brothers! Mary was commanded to say to them: "My Father and your Father, My God and your God." We are truly now one family. As believers we have the joy of knowing that we are a part of the family of God!

4) Mary obeyed: Mary came to the disciples and told them that she had seen the Lord. She then reported to them what Jesus had told her. Mark wrote that the disciples did not believe Mary Magdalene (Mark 16:11).

When we are faithful to go and tell, there will be those who do not believe. Our task is to be faithful, and leave the results in the hand of God. Mary was obedient. Jesus is looking for obedience in your life.

The agony and sorrow of Friday and Saturday must have seemed like an eternity to the disciples. But the pace of events increased rapidly with the coming of Easter morning. Mary came early to the tomb and found it empty. She ran and told Peter and John. They ran to the tomb. Mary followed. Mary met the Risen Lord. Jesus is alive! The grave could not hold Him! Satan could not defeat Him! Death had no power over Him!

The resurrection of Jesus draws all sincere seekers, summons all sufferers, and gives hope to all people. Dare we ask Jesus to make the miracle of the resurrection real in our lives today?

Some people can't find any joy in life because they are stuck on Friday. Does every day seen to be a cross day for you? You may be feeling the cross of suffering, feeling the nail prints of bereavement, or the calvary of painful memories. The only way to life and hope is to come to Jesus. Realize the tomb is empty and Jesus is alive!

EVENT 2: 'PETER AND JOHN RACED TO THE TOMB' (JOHN 20:3-10)

Resurrection Sunday all began with good news and running feet. The breathless Mary Magdalene raced back to tell Peter and John that the tomb was empty, and she did not know where the body of Jesus was. The younger John outran the older fisherman Peter to see for themselves if the story was true.

The question for us all these years later is, can we dare to hope, dare to believe, dare to shout "Hallelujah, Jesus is alive"?

PETER AND JOHN

1) Peter was the leader. "Mary ran and came to Simon Peter and to the other disciple whom Jesus loved ..." (John 20:2). In spite of Peter's denial, he was still the leader of the disciples. Peter had wept tears of repentance and had stayed in touch with the other disciples. All the others, except John, had fled that night in the garden. At least Peter had stayed and followed the arrested Jesus to the house of the high priest. Peter had failed. He had denied knowing Jesus three times. But Peter would become a "rock" in the early church.

2) Peter and John ran to the tomb. John was there with Peter when Mary arrived. We have said before that "the disciple whom Jesus loved" was most certainly John. Peter and John immediately set out for the tomb (John 20:3). They both were running. The younger John outran Peter and came to the tomb first (John 20:4).

John stopped on the outside of the tomb, "stooping down and looking in, saw the linen cloths lying there ..." (John 20:5). When Simon Peter arrived at the tomb, he went on into the tomb. He saw the linen cloths lying in the place where Jesus' body had been laid (John 20:6). The handkerchief that had been around the head of Jesus was "not lying with the linen cloths, but was folded together in a place by itself" (John 20:7).

3) Strips of cloths: Joseph of Arimathea and Nicodemus had wrapped the body of Jesus in linen cloths and had mixed a hundred pounds of myrrh and aloes in the cloths (John 19:39-40). John specifically wrote: "Strips of linen with the spices, as the custom of the Jews is to bury" (John 19:40). The Jews did not mummify bodies like the Egyptians. Bodies were wrapped with strips of linen cloth with spices and allowed to decay. Later, the bones were placed in a stone box in the tomb. The tomb then could be used again and again.

In recent years, much has been said on television about the "Shroud of Turin." It is a one-piece burial shroud supposedly used by Jesus. There is an imprint of a person's body on the shroud. However, this cannot have been used by Jesus because this is not the way the Jews cared for the dead. John specifically wrote "strips" of cloth, not a one-piece shroud (John 19:40). Also, three times John used the plural "cloths" (John 20:5-7).

4) John believed: John saw the same scene as Peter. Yet John believed (John 20:8). What did John see? When they entered the tomb, the cloth wrappings were all together. Jesus seemed to have passed through them. The linens were an empty shell, like a cocoon after the butterfly has flown away. The cloth that had covered the face of Jesus was "folded together in a place by itself" (John 20:7). John realized that no one had removed the body. Anyone would have taken the linens cloths and the spices. Jesus had passed through the cloths and was gone.

John commented that they did not yet know (remember the word "know" means to personally experience) or understand that Jesus would rise again from the dead (John 20:9). Then Peter and John left the tomb and went to their homes.

THE TRUTH OF THE RESURRECTION

Have you come to know and understand the truth of the

resurrection? Paul explained that if Jesus was not raised from the dead, there is no resurrection for anyone. We are all still lost in our sin. No hope. No heaven (1 Corinthians 15:12-17).

1) Responsibility: The truth of the resurrection will never dawn for you until you start taking responsibility for what happened Friday on the cross. Friday is our fault. We are responsible for our sin. We helped nail Jesus to the cross. But since Jesus died to pay the penalty for sin, there is no need for anyone to die in their sin anymore. Jesus paid the penalty for my sin, your sin, all sin! When we respond in faith to the grace of God offered to us because of the sacrifice of Jesus on the cross, our sin is forgiven.

It is easy for us to blame the Romans or the Jews for crucifying Jesus. You may think you can go on comfortable with the thought that it was a regrettable piece of history, but that you had no part in it.

2) Commitment: But if you could see the angry mob that cried out "crucify Him, crucify Him" as God saw it, you would discover your face in the crowd! Have you come to the place of faith in Jesus where you have entrusted your life and future into His hands? That is commitment. Have you trusted Jesus enough to follow Him and discover all the possibilities of service He has for you? When you are following the Risen Christ, our small differences will not seem insurmountable. You will realize that not only can Jesus change your life, but He can give you the power to be an overcomer.

3) Fears: The same Jesus who conquered death can conquer your fears. Jesus gives us hope. Without Jesus life is difficult at best and ends in death. But with Jesus, we have strength for living and the result is heaven and everlasting life.

Because of our Risen Savior, we know that someday broken lives will be healed, parted friends will be united, scars from old wounds will disappear, the hungry will be fed, swords will be turned into plows, and all the former things will pass away and all the tombs will be empty!

If pain, fear, disappointment, weariness or anger lie buried in your heart, they can be removed by our Lord Jesus Christ. Your salvation does not depend upon your good deeds or your heritage, but upon your faith in the Lord Jesus Christ, who arose from the dead.

Don't look for Jesus in a tomb. If you want to meet Jesus, you can right now. Put your faith in Jesus alone and you will never perish, but have everlasting life.

Event 3: 'The Disciples in the Upper Room' (John 20:1-23)

It was evening (between 3 and 6 p.m.) of Resurrection Sunday, and the disciples were assembled in the upper room (John 20:19). They had apparently continued to gather in the upper room where they had celebrated the Passover with Jesus. It was large enough for all of them to be together and mourn the loss of their Master. Mark wrote that they did not believe Mary Magdalene's report (Mark 16:11). So, at this point there were doubts concerning Jesus' resurrection.

Fear of the Jews

John wrote: "The doors were shut where the disciples were assembled for fear of the Jews" (John 20:19). The disciples had all witnessed the powerful force that arrested Jesus in the garden. They had heard accounts from Peter, John, Mary His mother, and the other women of the results of the terrible beatings and the crucifixion of Jesus.

They were now fearful for their own safety. They knew what the Jews did to Jesus, and they were thinking they might be next. Here in the United States we don't fear physical persecution. But in many places in the world churches are burned and Christians die for their faith. But as our nation continues to move toward a society that is more and more anti-God and anti-Christian, we may see our religious freedoms taken away. We, too, may face persecution.

JESUS IDENTIFIED HIMSELF

After Jesus greeted the disciples, "He showed them His hands and His side" (John 20:20). When Jesus appeared they might have thought it was His Spirit. But Jesus spoke and then He identified Himself. The way Jesus did that was to show His scars. Jesus showed them the nail prints in His hands and the scar in His side. The marks of the cross proved His identity. "Then the disciples were glad when they saw the Lord" (John 20:20).

Paul wrote of his identity in Christ: "From now on let no one trouble me, for I bear in my body the marks of the Lord Jesus" (Galatians 6:17).

We identify ourselves with a photo ID, like our driver's license. When you stand in the judgment, will you have identifying marks of the cross to show you are a follower of Jesus Christ? Has the Christ of the cross truly changed your life? When you came to the cross of Jesus, did that mark a change in your direction, a change in you?

JESUS COMMISSIONED THE DISCIPLES

Jesus again blessed the disciples with peace. And then Jesus said: "As the Father has sent Me, I also send you" (John 20:21). Notice that Jesus said: "As the Father has sent Me ... ." Jesus was sent into this world on a mission to bring forgiveness, mercy, and salvation to all who would repent of their sin, bow before Jesus as Lord. Jesus came in perfect obedience to His Father and came with the power and authority of God to accomplish God's will and purpose.

Jesus has charged His church to go into the world on a mission to proclaim forgiveness, mercy and salvation to all who would repent of their sins and bow before Jesus as Lord. Jesus said: "I also send you." We are to be obedient to the Lord Jesus and go forth under the authority of the Lord to accomplish His will and purpose. Just as Jesus was sent by the Father, we are sent by Jesus to be His representatives in the world. We are to carry on the mission that Jesus began. But we cannot do this under our own power. We need the power of the Lord working in us.

JESUS EMPOWERED HIS DISCIPLES

"He breathed on them, and said to them, 'Receive the Holy Spirit'" (John 20:22). Notice Jesus breathed on His disciples and gave them His Holy Spirit. In Genesis 2:7: "And the Lord God formed man of the dust of the ground, and breathed into his nostrils the breath of life; and man became a living being." The word for wind, breath, and spirit are the same in Hebrew. This is also true for the New Testament Greek word *pneuma*.

So when God first created man, He put His breath, His spirit in him. We are created in the image of God. When Jesus came to the disciples, He breathed into them His Holy Spirit in a new creation. Paul wrote: "Therefore, if anyone is in Christ, he is a new creation: old things have passed away; behold, all things have become new" (2 Corinthians 5:17). The disciples would be enabled to carry out the mission the Lord Jesus had given them.

THE DISCIPLES WERE TO PROCLAIM THE GOSPEL

Jesus said: "If you forgive the sins of any, they are forgiven them; if you retain the sins of any, they are retained" (John 20:23). This does not mean that on their own they could decide the sinful state or the forgiven state of any person. The church has the commission to proclaim the forgiveness of the Lord to all who come in repentance and faith to the Lord Jesus. But for those who do not repent and do not profess Jesus as

Lord, there is no forgiveness. "Nor is there salvation in any other, for there is no other name under heaven given among men by which we must be saved" (Acts 4:12). We have the power under God to proclaim forgiveness. We also have the power under God to warn those who reject Jesus that they are rejecting the mercy of God.

Our world today is filled with disastrous, dangerous, and discouraging events. But don't be discouraged. Keep trusting the Lord. No matter what the circumstances, or what others may do or say, keep believing in the Risen Lord. Since we have the good news about Jesus, tell it!

I read somewhere that John Wesley once said: "Give me one hundred men committed to God and we will storm the gates of hell!" So why aren't the gates of hell, the strongholds of Satan falling where you live? Why aren't they falling in your life? The answer lies in whether or not you are 100 percent sold out to Jesus Christ.

Jesus said: "And I, if I be lifted up from the earth, will draw all peoples to Myself" (John 12:32). As Jesus is lifted up, Satan will fall down! Our challenge is to lift Jesus up in our homes, in our churches, and in our cities!

EVENT 4: 'DOUBTING THOMAS' (JOHN 20:24-29)

If you were to search in a dictionary for the meaning of "doubt," it would be something like this: "One who habitually or instinctively questions." This tag has been stuck on Thomas down through the centuries. How would you like it if your name was attached to "doubt"? But was Thomas so much different from the rest of the disciples?

THE DISCIPLES

Jesus' mission in the world was to seek and to save the lost, and to reveal His Father and to die on the cross to pay the penalty for sin. Jesus gathered to Himself an inner circle of twelve disciples. This group became convinced that Jesus was the Messiah, sent to save Israel, defeat her enemies, and establish the kingdom. They traveled with Jesus, heard His teachings, and saw Him perform miracles. But they did not understand the true nature of the kingdom, nor the true purpose for which Jesus came. The hope of the disciples was dashed when Jesus was arrested and crucified. Except for John, they had all fled. Judas had betrayed Jesus, and Peter had denied Him.

The disciples did not understand that Jesus' death paid the penalty for sin. They did not understand that Jesus would be resurrected. The hope of the disciples was gone. The death of Jesus was a cruel ending to their dreams of an earthly kingdom.

But on Sunday morning, the women reported that the tomb was empty. Angels had told the women that Jesus was alive. Mary Magdalene said that she had seen the Risen Lord! But the disciples did not believe. Then Jesus came and appeared to the disciples in the upper room (John 20:19-23). Jesus invited them to see His hands and His side. Jesus sent forth His disciples as the Father had sent Him. Under the authority of Jesus, they were to proclaim the gospel to everyone. Jesus empowered the disciples with the Holy Spirit so they could accomplish their mission. But Thomas was not there.

THOMAS

"Now Thomas, called the Twin, one of the twelve, was not with them when Jesus came" (John 20:24). Thomas' problem was that he was absent! For an unknown reason Thomas was not present when Jesus appeared the first time to the disciples. Sometimes we have many excuses or reasons for not being present in worship with fellow Christians. The Scriptures' admonish us: "Not forsaking the assembling of ourselves together" (Hebrews 10:25).

When you are going through a difficult time for whatever reason, that's when you need the praying fellowship of believers more than ever. You may just want to be alone in sorrow, but the Lord can use the fellowship of the church to comfort you, strengthen you, and heal your heart.

Thomas could have been called "faithful" Thomas. When Jesus had told the disciples that He was going to Bethany because of Lazarus' illness, the disciples did not want to go. They knew the Jewish authorities wanted to kill Jesus. But Thomas spoke and said: "Let us go also, that we may die with Him" (John 11:16). Thomas had courage. Thomas loved Jesus. He had forsaken everything to follow Jesus. And he was loyal to the point of being willing to die with Jesus.

THE REPORT OF THE DISCIPLES

"The other disciples therefore said to him, 'We have seen the Lord'" (John 20:25). Thomas did not believe their report. He could not comprehend the truth of the resurrection. Thomas responded: "Unless I see in His hands the print of the nails, and put my finger into the print of the nails, and put my hand in His side, I will not believe" (John 20:25).

Was Thomas just being stubborn? He refused to believe the testimony of the other disciples. He had to see for himself. Have you ever been there? Is it hard for you to believe what others tell you? Remember, the other disciples had not believed until they had seen Jesus for themselves.

A possible problem was that Thomas was brokenhearted. Just like the other disciples, Thomas was discouraged and defeated. All hope was gone! His understanding of the kingdom was a failure! Perhaps Thomas felt like God had let him down.

Can you relate? Many people face the difficulties of life and give up hope. You may be facing financial problems, marriage problems, loss of mate, loss of a child, loss of a job, an illness, and the list could go on and on. When your problems are overwhelming, you are tempted to lose hope.

EIGHT DAYS LATER

"And after eight days His disciples were again inside, and Thomas was with them. Jesus came …" (John 20:26). Think about that! For eight days Thomas was left in his doubts. Why did Jesus make him wait? We don't know. Perhaps Jesus was breaking down the pride and self-reliance of Thomas. Perhaps He wanted Thomas to realize the limits of his reason or power. The Lord might make us wait for answers until we understand that we must "walk by faith and not by sight" (2 Corinthians 5:7).

Jesus appeared with the doors shut and stood in their midst, and Thomas was present (John 20:26). Jesus greeted the disciples like He had done the week before with the blessing of *shalom.*

Then Jesus spoke directly to Thomas: "Reach your finger here, and look at My hands; and reach your hand here, and put it into My side. Do not be unbelieving, but believing" (John 20:27).

Jesus did not rebuke Thomas or scold him or give him a lecture about not doubting. Jesus mercifully gave Thomas what he wanted. Jesus met Thomas right where he was. Basically Jesus said to him: "Touch Me and believe." Today, Jesus comes to you, right where you are and reveals His love to you in many ways. You can respond to the presence of the Lord and trust Him.

THOMAS RESPONDED TO JESUS

"And Thomas answered and said to Him, 'My Lord and my God!'" (John 20:28). We are not told whether Thomas actually touched Jesus or not. Thomas was face to face with Jesus. Thomas was offered the opportunity to touch Jesus. Thomas exclaimed: "My Lord and my God!"

Thomas is the first person in the gospels to confess Jesus as Lord and God. We should change the nickname of "Doubting Thomas" to "Believing Thomas." This was a genuine faith that flowed out of a heart healed by the presence of Jesus.

This strong statement of faith should characterize the lives of those who claim to follow Jesus. We should not be "ho hum" about our faith. "Churcheyanity" is not what Jesus is seeking. Jesus wants faithful followers. Has your soul ever cried out to Jesus as your Lord and your God?

JESUS GAVE US HOPE

"Thomas, because you have seen Me, you have believed. Blessed are those who have not seen and yet have believed" (John 20:29). This conclusion by Jesus is a word of encouragement for you and for all of us. We can't physically see Jesus now. But one day believers will see Jesus face to face. In the meantime, we must believe without seeing. The word "blessed" literally means "O the happiness of those." It doesn't mean that we are superior to others. It means that the Lord has chosen to pour out His love and grace. God sent His Son to die on the cross that all who believe in Him might have everlasting life.

Have you been blessed this way? Do you believe in Jesus as your Lord and God?

Jesus invites you to believe, just like He did Thomas.

Event 5: 'Gone Fishing'
(John 21:1-14)

It is impossible for us to know how the disciples were feeling because we have no record in Scripture. But the first heartbreak and sadness must have been erased where Jesus had appeared to them in the upper room. They knew Jesus was alive. But I don't think they understood what would come next. They did not know what to do without Jesus being there to physically lead them. They needed understanding. They needed leadership. They needed the power of Christ to move forward. It seems they were just waiting, not knowing how they should proceed, so Peter decided to go fishing (John 21:3).

Back to Their Old Job

This was not a simple holiday-type fishing trip. They had been professional fishermen, and they returned to the work they knew. John lists the nine disciples involved: Peter, Thomas, Nathanael, the sons of Zebedee (James and John) and two other disciples (John 21:2). They were in one of the large commercial boats that could accommodate that many men.

The night time was the best time for fishing on the Sea of Galilee (John 21:3). A large net with weights tied all around the edges would be cast out on the water. The weights would sink the net, and the men in the boat would then pull the net in. This process was repeated until enough fish had been caught. They worked all night and caught nothing (John 21:3).

When Jesus had called Peter and Andrew from their fishing business three years before, He said: "Follow Me, and I will make you fishers of men" (Matthew 4:19). But now they had returned to what they knew how to do: Fish for fish!

When Jesus called you, He called you to believe and follow Him. The desire of Jesus is that you would be a fisher of men. Jesus had already told the disciples in the upper room: "As the Father hath sent Me, I also send you" (John 21:21). We are to continue the work that Jesus started. With the power of His Holy Spirit within us, we are to seek and save the lost (Luke 19:10).

JESUS BY THE SEA

It was early morning, 3-6 a.m. (John 21:4). There was enough light that the disciples in the boat could see someone on the shore. The disciples did not know that it was Jesus (John 21:4). Jesus called out to them: "Children, have you any food?" (John 21:5). They answered "no." So the person on shore called to them and told them to cast their net on the right side of the ship, "and you will find some" (John 21:6).

Now, if you were a professional fisherman and you had not caught any fish after trying all night, how would you feel if someone on shore started giving you instructions about how to catch fish? You might be angry. You might think, "I'm the expert, what does he know?" Perhaps they were too tired to argue. "So they cast, and now they were not able to draw it in because of the multitude of fish" (John 21:6). They were unable to pull the net into their boat, so they rowed to shore dragging the net full of fish (John 21:8). When they reached the shore, they seemed to be amazed that the net was not broken (John 21:11).

RECOGNITION

Because of the instructions from the person on shore, and the resulting huge catch of fish, John realized the person on the shore was Jesus. John told Peter: "It is the Lord" (John 21:7). Simon Peter, always the impetuous one, grabbed his tunic and jumped in the water and swam to shore. The men would have removed their clothing, except for their loin cloths, in order to work with more freedom of movement. Peter wanted his tunic on when he greeted Jesus (John 21:7). The other disciples stayed in the boat, rowing ashore, dragging the heavy net full of fish (John 21:8).

When the disciples landed their boat, Jesus already had started a fire, had bread ready and was cooking fish (John 21:9). Jesus asked them to bring some of the fish they had caught (John 21:10). Jesus had everything prepared and invited the disciples to breakfast: "Come and eat breakfast" (John 21:12).

Just as Jesus invited the disciples, He invited us to join Him. He had made preparations. He has been fishing for souls, and He wants us to join Him in His work. None of them asked who He was, for they all knew it was Jesus (John 21:12). When you really know Jesus you will want to join Him in His work. Paul wrote: "For we are laborers together ..." (1 Corinthians 3:9).

Exact Number of Fish

John gave the exact number of fish to be 153 (John 21:11). We know that John used numbers symbolically. We have seen that here in John's gospel with the 7/7s! Remember, John is the author of the Revelation, and it has many numbers used symbolically. What, then, is the significance of the number 153? An early church leader, Jerome, wrote that in the Sea of Galilee there were 153 different kinds of fish. This would symbolize that one day people of all nations will be included in the kingdom of God. "After these things I looked, and behold, a great multitude which no one could number, of all nations, tribes, peoples, and tongues standing before the throne and before the Lamb clothed with white robes ..." (Revelation 7:9).

The Resurrected Lord

This event by the Sea of Galilee revealed the truth that Jesus was alive and not just a spirit or a vision of the disciples. The disciples did not see a vision on shore, they saw Jesus. A vision would not have pointed out where to cast the net to a group of professional fishermen. A spirit would not have caught fish, started a fire, prepared and cooked bread and fish. Jesus was alive, and He did all of these things.

Jesus took bread and gave it to them and He did the same with the fish (John 21:13). Serving the disciples in this manner should have reminded them of the last supper, the feeding of the multitude with the loaves and fish (John 6:11) and many shared meals. John reminded his readers that this was the third time Jesus revealed Himself to the disciples after the resurrection (John 21:14).

John wanted to make it clear that Jesus was alive. The same Jesus they had known, had traveled with, heard teach and preach, had seen do miracles, who had died on the cross was alive!

Jesus was back to give the church the power of the Holy Spirit and to commission the church to go into all the world teaching and preaching in the name of Jesus (Matthew 28:19-20).

This is our commission. This is our command. If you are not being obedient to this command of Jesus, you are either a disobedient disciple or not a disciple of Jesus at all.

With all the fish in the net, it did not break (John 21:11). The net could stand for the church. The church has room for all who will come! The church of the Lord Jesus Christ has room for all nations. There is no place for racial prejudice in the church. The love of God in Christ Jesus is available to all people. It is not about race, it is about grace. It is not your opinion that matters, but the witness of the mercy and love of God to all who will call upon His name.

Believers today should stand together beneath the cross of Christ and show to the world how we love one another and can live and work together. Only Jesus can make life like that possible.

EVENT 6: 'FOLLOW ME' (JOHN 21:15-19)

The conversation between Jesus and Peter by the Sea of Galilee is very striking for several reasons. Jesus questioned Peter three times about his love for Jesus. Peter responded three times with a different word for love. And Jesus gave Peter three commands. Jesus also revealed to Peter the type of death he would face, and then gave Peter a final challenge: "Follow Me" (John 21:19).

QUESTION ONE

1) Jesus' question: Jesus asked Peter, "Do you love Me?" (John 21:15). Jesus used the verb form of *agape* for "love." This word was associated with God's kind of love. It describes a selfless love. A love that wants what is best for the other person. Remember, Peter had denied knowing Jesus three times on the night that Jesus was arrested and taken before Caiaphas. So by the Sea of Galilee, Jesus asked Peter three times if he loved Him.

2) Jesus added: "More than these?" (John 21:15). Was Jesus referring to things like the fishing boat and nets? Peter had gone back to his fishing business. Did he love Jesus more than his career? Or perhaps Jesus referred to the other disciples. Did Peter really love Jesus more than the others? Peter had once bragged that he did: "I will lay down my life for Your sake" (John 13:32). Peter also said: "Even if all are made to stumble, yet I will not be" (Mark 14:29). Perhaps Jesus meant both. Did Peter love Him more than the others and more than his fishing business? What about you? Do you love Jesus more than your career?

Do you love Jesus more than the things this world offers?

3) Peter's response: Peter responded to the question by saying: "Yes, Lord, You know that I love You" (John 21:15). When Peter responded to Jesus, he did not use the same word for "love" that Jesus used. Jesus used the verb form *agape*, which is the most powerful word for "love" in the Greek language. Peter responded with the verb form of the Greek word *philos*, which means "brotherly love." The city of Philadelphia contains this word and means the "city of brotherly love." Perhaps Peter was admitting that he knew that his love for Jesus did not equal the love of Jesus for him.

4) The command of Jesus: Jesus commanded Peter to "feed My lambs" (John 21:15). Lambs are not full-grown, mature sheep. Jesus commanded Peter to assume the role of the shepherd, the pastor to care for the young and immature believers.

QUESTION TWO

1) Jesus' question: Jesus asked a second time: "Simon, son of Jonah, do you love Me?" (John 21:16). Jesus again asked Peter if he had God's kind of love, a selfless love, for Him. Jesus used again the verb form of the word *agape*.

2) Peter's response: Again, Peter was not able to use the word for love which Jesus had used. Peter responded: "You know I have 'brotherly love' for You" (John 21:16).

3) The command of Jesus: Jesus then commanded Peter to "tend My sheep" (John 21:16). "Sheep" would have referred to the entire flock of sheep regardless of age. The word "tend" was the common word for the work of the shepherd. A shepherd "tended" his sheep. The shepherd led his sheep to grass and water, protected them from wild animals and robbers, and nursed their wounds. The shepherd also went after the lost sheep that wandered away.

QUESTION THREE

1) Jesus' question: Jesus asked a third time: "Simon, son of Jonah, do you love Me?" (John 21:17). But this time Jesus did not use the word *agape* for love. Jesus switched and used the word Peter had been using. So Jesus asked: "Simon, son of Jonah, do you have "brotherly love" for Me?" It seems that Jesus lowered His expectations of Peter. Jesus met Peter at his level. Did Peter really have "brotherly love" for Jesus?

2) Peter's response: Peter was grieved that Jesus asked him the third time: "Do you have 'brotherly love' for Me?" (John 21:17). I believe Peter was grieved for two reasons. One reason was that Jesus asked the question three times. This could have brought back to Peter's mind the painful experience of denying his Lord three times. The second reason is that Jesus switched to the word Peter had been using for "love."

Peter said: "Lord, You know all things." That is a wonderful admission that we all need to make. Jesus knows all things! Peter continued: "You know that I have brotherly love for You" (John 21:17).

3) The command of Jesus: Jesus commanded: "Feed My sheep" (John 21:17). One of the primary duties of the shepherd was to make sure his sheep were fed. One of the primary duties of any pastor or Christian teacher is to be certain they are presenting faithfully the Word of God to their listeners. People's souls are truly nourished as they study prayerfully the Bible.

PETER'S DEATH FORETOLD

Jesus told Peter there would come a time when he was old that he would no longer be in control of his situation. "You will stretch out your hands, and another will gird you and carry you where you do not wish to go" (John 21:18). Jesus revealed to Peter the type of death that Peter would face. Peter's death would glorify God (John 21:19). The phrase "stretch out your hands" probably referred to crucifixion.

Jesus then gave Peter the challenge He had given him three years before: "Follow Me" (John 21:19). That is the same challenge Jesus gives to each of us. Are you willing to follow in the footsteps of Jesus?

There is a cost to discipleship. When we respond to the Lord's command to follow Him, there is a cost involved. "Then Jesus said to His disciples, 'If anyone desires to come after Me, let him deny himself and take up his cross and follow Me … whoever loses his life for My sake will find it'" (Matthew 16:24-25).

Have you taken up your cross and followed Jesus? We find life when we are willing to lose it for the cause of Christ.

EVENT 7: 'WHAT ABOUT JOHN?' (JOHN 21:20-25)

When you study the New Testament, the focus is on the Lord Jesus Christ. But there are three people who stand out as followers of the Lord. One was Peter, the recognized leader of the disciples. His strength and determination were key ingredients that Jesus used to shape Peter into the leader of the early church. Paul, who met Jesus on the Damascus Road, was dramatically changed by his encounter with the Lord. Paul became the most powerful evangelist and missionary of the early church. Not only did he spread the gospel around the Roman Empire, his letters became a major part of the New Testament. I think the third most influential leader in the early church was John, the beloved disciple. John wrote the Gospel of John, three letters included in the New Testament, and the Book of Revelation. John was a thinker and writer used by the Lord to express the truth of the gospel to all people, especially the Gentiles.

PETER AND JOHN

After Jesus had challenged Peter to "follow Me" (John 21:19), Peter turned and saw John following behind them (John 21:20). John is again described by the phrase: "the disciple whom Jesus loved." There is also the reminder that this disciple was the one leaning on Jesus as they reclined around the low table at the last supper. Peter had asked John to ask Jesus: "Lord, who is the one who betrays You?" (John 21:20).

Peter was apparently concerned about John's role in the kingdom, so Peter asked: "But Lord, what about this man?" (John 21:21).

JESUS' RESPONSE

"If I will that he remain till I come, what is that to you?" You follow Me" (John 21:22). There are several important truths contained in this verse.

1) *"If I will"*: Jesus had a purpose for Peter and a purpose for John. Jesus has a purpose, a will for all of us. We can rebel, turn away from Jesus and refuse to follow His will for our lives. The Lord created us with a free will. We are not robots, with our decisions out of our hands. We have choices. In the Garden of Eden, all was perfect in God's creation. God told Adam and Eve not to eat the fruit of a certain tree. They rebelled, they disobeyed God and ate fruit from that tree. Sin and death entered because of disobedience.

2) *"What is that to you?"* Jesus told Peter plainly that it was not his concern what He wanted John to do. We should have care for others. We should care for their needs. We should seek to help those in need with the resources that we have been blessed with by the Lord. Most of all we should care about whether or not they know the Lord Jesus as their personal Savior.

But it is not our task to determine the will of God for some other believer's life. We do not have the wisdom or the authority to control another person's life. Only Jesus has the wisdom and authority to lay out the path He wants each of us to take. We all must trust Jesus and pray for one another that we would be in the center of His will for our lives.

3) "You follow Me." Again, Jesus had to remind Peter that his job was to focus on what Jesus wanted him to do and not be distracted from his purpose by wondering about John.

I know some people who can multitask. But it is truly rare for a person to do two things really well at the same time. We need to have our focus on Jesus and a single-mindedness about obeying His will for our lives. With so many distractions in our world, it may be difficult, but we are called to focus on Jesus and follow Him: "[A]nd let us run with endurance the race that is set before us, looking unto Jesus, the author and finisher of our faith ..." (Hebrews 12:1-2).

4) John's explanation: This conversation between Jesus and Peter about John spread among the brethren that John would not die. John wanted to correct this misunderstanding. John explained that Jesus did not say he would not die but: "If I will that he remain till I come, what is that to you?" (John 21:23).

John's Concluding Statements

1) John acknowledged that he testified of these things and wrote these things and that he was telling the truth (John 21:24).

2) John said that if everything Jesus said and did were written down, he supposed the world could not hold all the books that would be written (John 21:25). John was selective in showing the essence of Jesus' teaching, examples of His healing power, how Jesus related to people and the authorities. John did all of this in order to demonstrate that Jesus was the Son of God.

3) John explained his purpose clearly: "And truly Jesus did many other sign in the presence of His disciples, which are not written in this book; but these are written that you may believe that Jesus is the Christ, the son of God, and that believing you may have life in His name" (John 20:30-31). Amen!

CPSIA information can be obtained
at www.ICGtesting.com
Printed in the USA
LVHW030902130721
692557LV00009B/752

9 781955 295017